Rafael dos Santos

MOVING

ONE STEP AT A TIME

Real stories and advice to help you succeed

Moving Abroad - One Step at a Time

First published in 2013 by

Panoma Press
48 St Vincent Drive, St Albans, Herts, AL1 5SJ, UK

info@panomapress.com
www.panomapress.com

Book layout by Neil Coe

Printed on acid-free paper from managed forests. This book is printed on demand to fulfill orders, so no copies will be remaindered or pulped.

ISBN 978-1-908746-97-9

Dedication

I want to dedicate this book to my sister Andiara who shared her thoughts before returning to Brazil and during her reverse culture shock process.

To my partner William who was always there, with a cup of tea, during the late nights while I was writing.

And my parents for having done whatever they could to provide me with the tools to develop my career and my life. I love you both.

Acknowledgement

I wish to thank all my friends who have shared their stories and experiences with me and have dedicated their precious time in many different ways to help me to finalise this book.

A big thank you to Carrie Lau, Paul Barnes, Carlos Kytka, Sileide Santos, Alina Zegheru, Iain Speirs, Tiina Vlio, Richard Williams, Abilio Esteves, Bruno Lincoln, Nisha Rubabha, Chris Orlikowski, Lisa Pattenden, Fredrik Bjarnason, Stefan Arestis, Chris Redhead, Leonardo Medeiros, Katia Barria, Monika Lazlo and Lui Savi.

Very special thanks to Vagner Araujo and Doreen Werner.

Contents

Stage 1 - The Decision

Stage 2 - Research

Stage 3 - Moving

Stage 4 - The upgrade

Stage 5 - Direction

Introduction

Welcome abroad!

The journey of going abroad can be a challenge.

If you are reading this book, you probably have been thinking for a long time about going to another country or you plan to go soon.

Once you have made the decision, I can help to make your journey easier and much more fun!

What I have done is break down this journey into 5 stages, each stage having its own challenges, concerns, achievements and emotions.

You do not have to worry about which stage you are going through. It will be a natural transition from one to another. You cannot go from stage 1 to 5 without going through stage 3!

From the moment you decide to go away to the moment you return home, the process is the same. From Vietnam to Brazil or the USA to India, you will go through an amazing journey where you will meet great people, eat delicious diverse foods, discover fantastic places and make friends for a lifetime!

What stops you from going on this journey is yourself!

So, if you have any doubts about your trip, be prepared to start your journey right now, from the moment you start reading Chapter 1.

This book will not help you to decide where to go. It is not a guidebook. It does not give tips on countries or destinations.

This book helps you to get through the journey (both physical and emotional) when you have already chosen to go abroad.

You will be reading several true stories about the experiences my friends and I went through and decided to share with the world, including YOU!

STAGE 1

The Decision

CHAPTER 1

The Decision

Deciding to travel abroad is the first stage, in which you'll be wondering how things are going to be in another country, what your life is going to be like.
This stage is full of the fear and excitement of the unknown and all the other feelings related to going to an adventure.

There are 3 main points in the Decision stage:

1 – Where you are going? - Place
2 – When you are going? - Date and time
3 – Why you are going? - Reason or goal for the trip

In many cases, I believe that where and why are linked. If you want to learn English, for example, you travel to English speaking countries like the UK, the USA, Australia, Canada, etc.

So, you can connect the 'why' you are going with the 'where' you are going. Once you make this connection, you just need to decide 'when'.

Sometimes 'when' is decided by 'how much'. If you are going to a country where the currency is twice or three times the currency of your country, you will need more time to save money.

Reasons that people go to another country

When you decide to move away – whatever length of time – you should have a goal. It will help you to keep sane and ensure you make the best of your time abroad.

During several hundreds of hours of conversation with people from different countries, I have learnt that every single story has a meaning. Everyone will have a different reason why they have made the decision to leave everything behind and try the unknown.

Some answers I hear most are:

Change of air

This is a very common response. It really depends on the age (average age: 30's). They need to think about their lives, they need to move on, meet new people and learn something new to be able to progress in their lives. Normally, they already have a stable career but need a new challenge. People who need a 'change of air' are usually bored with their lives (at least the people that I spoke to).

Education

Some people want to learn a new language for personal or professional reasons. This also involves obtaining a degree, whether as an undergraduate or graduate student or any other type of higher education, which will lead to a better position in their own country. If the right opportunity comes along, they can stay where they are or even move to wherever the job will take them.

Career development

Some people go abroad to work (or even volunteer) in their field so they can gain international experience.

There are also those people who decide that they actually do not like their current job and turn their lives upside down with a new job or even a new business idea. They see other businesses, talk to people who love their careers and their passion make them realise there is more to life than money.

Broken heart

I can't tell you how many 'broken hearts' I've met along the way. People in long-term relationships frequently need to detach themselves completely from the place and people so they are able to move on. They need a break from their world so they 'throw themselves' into a completely new journey so they can find themselves free again. This is where the saying goes 'out of sight, out of heart'.

Explore the world

Many of those who are excited about geography or history decide they need to see the world with their own eyes – all the battles and wars that occurred in those magnificent places. I felt quite emotional the first time I went to Berlin and saw pieces of the wall that had divided the city. Although it was not part of my own history, I mourned for those who lived during that time and had to suffer as they did.

Expand your knowledge

Exploring the world will lead to expanding your knowledge – no doubt about that. It will make you a 'new' person. You will learn things that you can only learn if you are actually there. I was in Poland in 2003 for Christmas and I learnt about their traditional Christmas celebration. They go to the market the day before to choose the carp (fish) that will be on the table on Christmas day. Even if my Polish friends have told me about the tradition, it would have not been the same. I was there; I chose the fish and I saw the preparation. We had to wait until the first star appeared in the sky to start eating. The experience was unique and I fondly remember it as if it was today.

To improve yourself as a human being

Travel will make you more patient, more knowledgeable and will make you a better human being. You will better understand things and be more compassionate, especially if you travel to under- developed countries. You will see that people are happy even in poverty and that they learn to deal with that on a daily basis. Unless you also come from a very poor background, the experience will change the way you see food and material possessions

To make it

This is normally the reply from very ambitious people. You move somewhere else because where you live, it is either very difficult 'to make it' or the conditions will never be favourable for you to reach your goal. 'To make it' means to reach your goal or objective. For example, suppose that you want to become a famous fashion designer. If your country does not provide the tools (either peoples' mind or the economy is too poor for people to spend money on clothes), you go somewhere else to create your label.

To find love

Funny as it sounds, people really go in search for love. For whatever reason they cannot find their other half in their own country, so they go somewhere else so they have a better chance. I remember a ginger (red-haired) friend of mine saying how much she loved Brazil. I asked her why and she said: 'I never had so much attention in my life. There are almost no ginger girls in Brazil so I was exotic. I was chatted up a lot by very attractive men'. I thought this was very funny but after 6 months, she said she was preparing to move to Brazil. She said she was going to find love there and now – 7 years later – she's married.

These are just a few examples. Many of these reasons will end up adding to each other and even if your goal was to learn the language, you will end up being more knowledgeable, bettering yourself in some way, changing the atmosphere, etc.

Keep this reason in mind, the main reason that you are going.

A lot of my friends have different ways to describe their journeys but they all agree on so many things and realise that even if they are from different countries and have different goals, their stories are frequently the same.

Real stories behind the reasons...

When you move to another country, you will meet people from all over the world. You will spend a lot of time with your new friends and there will always be something new to learn. Make the most of it. Do not criticise; just take in every experience and if you think that will add to your life, adopt the idea or share it.

I once met a girl named Nisha from Bangladesh. The first time I met her (through Bangladeshi friends), she was very shy and barely said anything. I had had contact with other Bangladeshi women previously when I did an interpreting course in 2004. I knew they are not very talkative, so this was the impression I had about all Bangladeshi girls, but maybe that was just me generalising – which is wrong.

A few months later, I met Nisha again; she had changed dramatically and seemed happier, more enthusiastic and had 'more life'.

We had an opportunity to talk and I realised that first impressions really should not count. Nisha was probably being herself this time and I asked her why she was so quiet and shy when I first met her. She explained that she had just arrived from Bangladesh and she was not very confident. She needed to explore the city and understand the culture before she could flourish. She was probably overwhelmed by the differences between London and Bangladesh.

During our conversation, I asked her why she moved to London. Most people would simply say 'for work' or 'to study' or 'to do this and that' and then they would expand on the reason in more detail.

Nisha actually told me her life story, which was very emotional and revealed a great deal about her character. Her very polite manners and well-spoken English made me realise that she came from a family that valued education and manners. One thing from our conversation that stayed in my mind was:

'I was a very bright student through my life. I got many scholarships and awards, which helped me to continue my studies further. As I am the eldest child of my family, I am the 'heart' of my father. He encouraged me and supported me to come to London to further my studies and invested his money in me. The reasons I came to London are to make money for my father's operation, to give better education to my little brothers, to build a house for my family, to ensure good food in every meal they take. Finally, to complete my education with a first class degree'.

I was very touched and kept thinking 'how can someone so fragile be so ambitious and determined to succeed?'

That's when I learned another lesson. How you are really does not matter: shape, size, colour or religion - when you have a goal. Even though her family was on the other side of the world and she was sharing a room in a flat with another Bangladeshi girl in order to save money, she had a very firm goal.

This made her trip much easier (in some ways). Being determined to achieve led her to look for jobs related to her work (she wanted to become an accountant). She was also living in a flatshare and sharing a room – and I knew all that very well as I had been in the same situation when I first moved to London.

When I arrived in London the first time, I lived in a house with 14 people and there were four of us in the room. I learned that 'personal space' was only my own bed. We each had two drawers for our clothes. It was a very different situation from sharing my flat with one other friend in Sao Paulo, Brazil.

Another friend of mine who comes from a working class family in Brazil also shared his story:

'I was 18 when I left Brazil for the first time to live in Europe. I immigrated for educational and ideological reasons and to improve my language and academic skills. I lived in five cities in different countries where I had diverse experiences and also I learned a lot from them. Before going to Portugal, the first country I lived, I spent all my childhood and adolescence living with my parents who never taught me how life is beyond our front door.

When I arrived in Portugal, I found out my mum was not there to organise the house such as washing the dishes, doing the laundry, ironing my clothes, cleaning the house, going shopping and so on. These tasks made a big difference when I started sharing accommodation with more experienced people who had already lived without parents or housemaids for a long time. Those flatmates taught me how to comply with my responsibilities as tenant, which prepared me for the next place where I lived in Barcelona.

In Catalonia, people's mentality is so different compared to those in Brazil or Portugal. I identified with the Catalan culture in all aspects. I knew I would live there for a long time. I subscribed to a website where I contacted a woman who was letting rooms at reasonable price so I rented a room from her.

In order to adapt myself quicker to the culture and integrate myself in Catalan society, I enrolled myself in a Catalan language intensive course, which I attended during the 2-hour break that I had while working in a restaurant.

After one year living in Barcelona, I was already enrolled in a superior technician course to get access to higher education. During my studies, I was selected to do an internship in Rome for two months, where I lived in order to complete the course.

It was one of the best experiences I had in my life. Unforgettable moments lived with great people. A lot of experience was acquired during that time and one of most important, I got fluent in Italian with just a short time practising with Italian friends and self-learning books.

Among the differences between the countries I lived, I can highlight the food, which varies from country to country, people's lifestyle such as sleeping after lunch time (in Spain, for example, they sleep from 2pm to 5pm) during a working day then going out late as many clubs in Latin countries like Spain, Portugal and Italy close later (compared to the UK and Northern European countries) and undoubtedly the development and organisation in general.

The main thing that I learned is that mistakes will make you stronger. Learn with them. Do not beat yourself up because you made a mistake. Learn a lesson and move on quickly. Do not waste time thinking over and over about the mistake.

If you are moving to another country, try to learn the culture beforehand. These days, there are videos, blogs and groups where you can learn before you get there so it's much easier for you to integrate.'

Start writing your own story!

Now, to make sure you have a clear picture of what, where and when, write down – here on this page – your Stage 1 plan:

Where you are going:

....

....

....

When you are going (date and time):

....

Why are you going?

Take time to think about it. Be honest with yourself and reflect on all the reasons that you are going and what you want to achieve. What are your goals? What are your objectives? You can get a separate sheet if you want to, but try to keep within the book so you can always refer to it (Later on in the book, there will be references to this chapter again).

....

....

....
....
....
....
....
....
....
....
....
....
....
....
....
....
....
....
....
....
....
....
....
....

Dealing with your emotions while still planning your trip

You'll encounter your first emotions when you buy your airplane ticket.

It feels like 'there is no way back' – unless, of course, you want to pay cancellation charges – but this is not what you are thinking about!

You are excited, very excited!

It is probably your first trip abroad or even the first time you are going to leave your family for a long period of time.

There is so much going through your mind that you almost feel overwhelmed and you don't know where to start.

Do Not Panic! There is time for everything!

This stage of your trip is planned about 6 months prior to your leaving (in most cases). You have already made the decision to move (or go away for a year or many years) and now you need to think about the practicalities.

Barriers

You must be careful when talking to people so they don't put you off. Some people are going to be very sceptical about your idea and your new journey. They will give you 1000 reasons why it is dangerous, not good, bad, horrible, and any other negative adjective you can think of. It is up to you whether or not you are going to listen to them and take their advice on board.

Remember that every journey is unique. Even if they have been to another country and it was a terrible experience, it was THEIR experience and not YOURS.

Make your own story!

At one time, I was travelling around Eastern Europe on my Brazilian passport with a Scottish friend. We were going from Poland to Austria. I don't know what happened, but we got on the wrong train and ended up in Czech Republic. I didn't have the right visa so when the train stopped on the border, two huge immigration officers with guns bigger than me escorted me off the train.

It was 2am and I had to wait for two hours until the next train back to Poland. It was December and the temperature on the platform was -17C (yes, minus 17!). I had a skiing mask to protect my face from the cold and I was so terrified that I cried. The tears froze on the mask and became ice. It was a frightening experience but I don't tell people not to travel because of that. You will have your own funny stories to tell – hopefully, not many terrifying ones.

So, do not let yourself be put off by the negativity of people around you. Make sure you make the most of your trip and have the time of your life!

First things first!

The practicalities you need to consider

Bank account
If you have decided to go for a short period (maybe up to 1 year), you need to think if it's worth keeping your bank account open in your home country. In some countries, you have to pay monthly fees and other taxes on your account, so if you are not going to be using it at all, you can either close or suspend the account for a period of time. It's always worth checking what the options are. Talk to your bank manager and they normally can advise the best steps. Many banks are international or have agreements with other banks so they can help you to open a bank account in the country where you are going, so it's worth checking if your bank can do the same.

Mobile phone
If you have a monthly payment plan, can you close it or suspend it or transfer the account to someone else, so you don't have to pay?

Health insurance
There are different issues here:

If you have private health insurance in your country and are going way for a year, will it cover you abroad?

Check the policy and be sure you have their international phone numbers (especially in the country where you are going) and your policy number at all times.

Once I travelled to France and had a skiing accident. Luckily, I had everything saved on my phone on my contact list. Paperwork was dealt with within minutes. Nothing really serious happened but it was certainly good to have all the details in hand. They would have charged me over US$1000 (one thousand American dollars to remove me by ski ambulance and take me to hospital for x-rays).

If you have a chronic illness, you may need daily medication. Will you be able to buy medication for the whole year while you are away? If you need a cream or a pill, can you buy in the country where you are going? Will you be able to go to hospital or see a doctor who can prescribe your medication if you need it?

I have a family member who needs medication on her skin every 3 months so she had it delivered while she was away on a course for 18 months. Her mum used to send via DHL. That's also an option to be considered.

Travel insurance
If you are one of the new techi-people who loves a gadget (like me!), you should consider investing in travel insurance. There's nothing worse than losing your camera or phone while you are away, right?

Just so you know, when you travel, your mind is not in the right place . . . what I mean is that when you are in a new place, a new environment because everything is new and you don't have a routine yet, it is very likely that you will lose things. You will drop them, leave them on the bus or train – especially if you are chatting on the phone! Bags will stay behind. If you moving from a hot country to a cold country, you will not be accustomed to the weather and wearing so many layers of clothes so you will most probably lose your wallet, keys, etc. It happened to me and to most of my friends the first 3 months after they had moved. In the office, for example, having to call back our clients to say they forgot their passport or ID after they signed a contract is very normal. Their minds are so busy and worried about finding a home, a job, etc., that they end up forgetting things.

It does not mean you are 'stupid' or forgetful. It only means that you are not yet accustomed to the environment.

Electric devices

Different countries have different voltage and different plug sizes and shapes. There's no standard size or shape (like USBs), which makes life more difficult if you are travelling. There are several international adapters for you to choose from that normally come with different shapes of plugs.

Items like phone chargers, electric razors, etc. will need an adapter or even a small transformer to be used in another country.

Documents

Most the countries that I have visited have adopted some sort of ID card (the size of credit card). The UK still uses either the driver's license or passport as identification. Brazil, Spain, Italy, France and most European counties have some sort of identification.

What happens when you lose them?

Make sure you know the address of the consulate of your country as well as the embassy.

I almost forgot: don't forget you will need your passport; be sure to check how to get a new one in case you lose yours! Have spare photographs in case you need emergency passports or IDs.

In 2000, I travelled abroad for the first time, spending a week in France and then moving on to London. During my first week in London, I lost my wallet with my Brazilian ID cards, credit cards, driver's license, etc. (I believe they fell from my pocket on the bus while I was speaking to someone on my mobile phone.)

I didn't renew them because I was planning to stay in London for a long time. The surprise came when I needed to renew my passport (5 years later). I went to the Embassy to find out how to get my new documents and learnt that someone had found and turned in my documents; they had kept them for 5 years. I was happy and surprised at the same time. So if you lose yours, try to find them in Lost and Found property of the bus company as well as train or underground companies.

It took me no time to renew my passport and I never lost my documents again – from that date onward, I only carry a copy of my IDs!

Another thing that I did was to scan all my documents and store them in my email, just in case I needed a copy again.

Travel list

I believe the list below contains all the items that you should think about for your trip.

See what you will need (or not) and get them into your suitcase!!

You can print this list off from our Facebook page: www.facebook.com/roominthemoon

Legal Documentation

- Print two copies of all documentation (credit cards, licence, passport, visa, tickets, hotel invoice, insurance, vaccinations); leave one at home and put one in your luggage.

- Have the contact details of your country's consulate and embassy in both your email and in print.

- Passport

- Visa (make sure you have all your documentations related to your visa sorted)

- Apply for International driver's license

- If you have credit cards, let the credit card companies know you are going to use them abroad and where.

- Travel cheques or money in the currency where you are going. It is advisable to take small notes and coins so you can pay for the taxi, train, etc.

Health

- Vaccinations – if you need them for the country where you are going.

- Health documentation – if you have any sort of allergy, epilepsy, etc.

- Prescriptions – (pills, creams, etc.) Also check if your doctor can prescribe in the language where you are going and if it's going to be accepted there.

- Prepare a first aid kit (bandages, band aids, aspirin, antacid tablets, antibiotic cream, insect repellent, sunscreen, towelettes, ear plugs, sewing kit)

Insurance

- Travel Insurance and all contact details (including the phone number for the country where you are going)
- Medical insurance

Reservations

- Airport transfer phone number (if you booked one)
- Any other type of reservation (if you are travelling by boat, kayak, car, bus, etc.)
- Accommodations: name of the place, address, phone number, directions, map
- Car rental reservations (address, car location, telephone number and reservation number)

House and home

- Pet – if you have one, who will be looking after it?
- Magazine subscription cancellation
- Provide a copy of your itinerary to your parents AND best friend (if he or she is not travelling with you, of course!).
- Leave a house key with someone you trust (if you live alone or if you are not renting your house out).

- All bills to be paid and cancelled
- Ask a friend, family or neighbour to check calls on answering machine and clear them
- Remove the food from cupboard and fridge/ freezer.

Destination

- Guidebooks
- Make a list of things to do in the city where you are moving.
- Cash – local currency and in the country where you are going
- Check weather (so you know what type of clothes to take with you)
- Get familiar with some local laws (especially linked to immigration) so you know your rights
- Learn to say the basics: please, thank you, excuse me, and so on.
- Travel games (so you don't get bored on the plane?)

Electronics

- Camera: any type: camcorder, photo, etc.
- Chargers: for all your equipment
- Charge all your equipment before your flight.
- Batteries (if you need any)
- Laptop (card, cable, battery, etc.)

- Mobile phone (charger and spare battery if possible - also make sure it's fully charged)
- Adapter plug
- MP3 player (charged, with cable and battery)

On the airplane

- A book, magazine or any other reading material
- Neck support (if you are flying economy, you will need one!)
- Bottled water
- Ear plugs
- MP3 player

Clothes

The type of clothes you are going to wear will depend on the weather of the country where you are going. The list below is just a reminder of the items you might need.

- Trousers or pants (depending on if you speak American or British English)
- Shorts
- Long sleeve tops
- Short sleeved tops
- Light jacket (feather down are very lightweight)
- Evening tops/dresses (female) shirts (male)
- Socks
- Sandals and flip flops

- Trainers / Sneakers / comfortable walking shoes
- Shoes for going out
- Hat
- Underwear for every day away
- Have underwear in your hand luggage in case your suitcase gets lost

Other items

Depending on the type of trip that you are going, you may need:

- Toiletries: moisturiser, eye cream, hand cream, body cream, deodorant, talc, shampoo, conditioner, toothpaste, tampons, razors, shaving cream, after shave, makeup, perfume, hair brush, comb, small hairspray, hair dryer
- Binoculars, suitcases/rucksacks, backpack, alarm clock, coil heater, cup, instant coffee, umbrella, laundry bag, charged toothbrushes, refilled bathroom things, including matches, plastic bags for general use, a list of people you need to buy gifts for, beach or bath towel, flannel/hand towel, folding raincoat, poncho, sunglasses, and anything else that you can think of that will be useful for your trip!

STAGE 2

RESEARCH

CHAPTER 2

Research

Researching for your new home and work online

If this is the first time you've looked for a place to live away from your home country, there are many things that you need to take in consideration.

If you are not sure about booking your accommodation online via websites like londonup.com, do not panic. You are not alone. You just have to be careful when booking online.

My tips are:

- Check the website credentials (are they registered with any government body?)
- Is this website recommended or mentioned by other people on chat rooms, forums, etc.?
- Can you actually contact anyone who has used this site before?

These are some ways to be sure that the information is legitimate. You can also call to see if the number has been listed correctly.

Before booking for a long-term stay, you can also reserve a few nights in a hotel, hostel or apartment.

On the group page, you will be able to ask the other travellers for tips on where to find accommodations.

Of course, I can strongly recommend londonup.com if you want book a room directly before you do a viewing. I founded the company myself and I know the property market in London inside and out, so you can trust my referral!!

You may feel hesitant when you start searching. How do you know that property actually exists and it's not just a bogus ad to take your money? You need reassurance that it will be okay. You will be somewhere completely new; if the room is not there, you don't have friends or family to run to. If you are suddenly on the street, it will be much more expensive if you have to find a hotel that night!

Truth is, you don't really know. Because we actually manage the properties, booking via londonup.com ensures that you will definitely have a room when you arrive. Search for websites that are similar and then search for online reviews about them.

This may be a daunting task but it's crucial that your research is thorough and you learn about the city, the area and neighbourhood where you are going to be staying (if you already have an idea where you are going to stay).

There are so many websites that can provide useful information about places these days, like tripadvisor.com, where you can literally find a review about everything everywhere.

Just make sure you search in your own language and in English. Once you have selected a few places, you can either contact them from your location through Skype, email, phone or Facebook, or short-list them to visit when you arrive.

You will feel lost at the beginning but after two or three searches, you will get the hang of it and will be a pro in searching for the perfect new pad!

How do you choose the right place?

Ok, so if you are abroad, I would suggest that you not sign anything or pay a large amount of money upfront.

If you can see the site is trustworthy, there is an address and you can see reviews or comments about the agency or the landlord online, then you should contact them.

If you have booked a hotel, a hostel or a room with londonup.com, you will have more time to search for the perfect place. You may even end up staying in the accommodation that you found online if it seems good. That will save you a lot of time and hassle searching for another place.

Make sure you bookmark the pages that you find interesting; they will be useful.

If you want to ensure that you don't forget them, write them down in this book.

Work

How do you search for work online?

Well, there are so many websites where you can find this information but don't forget people will invite you for interviews. You need to note on your curriculum vita or the application that you are still in your country and will be moving to their location on 'this date'.

Culturally speaking, people in different countries have different ways of hiring and ask different questions. You need to do your research and be culturally prepared for certain questions.

In Brazil, for example, they ask about your future (do you plan to get married, to have kids, etc.). (I am not sure if the law has changed now).

YouTube has millions of videos that you can use to research. It's worth checking.

Now, you can create your own list of websites and what they include:

Website	Content
Example: londonup.com	Accommodation in London

Where to stay before you move to your own room or flat

Staying with a friend

Let's make things very clear about staying with a friend ...

They may be living in a shared house and normally, flatmates have no problem with friends staying for a few days (I repeat: a few days!). For some people, a few days means two, for others, five and for some people, a few does not have a number ...

There is a proverb in Brazil that says: 'guests are like fish; after 3 days, they go off.' - do you get the meaning?

I have a few tips if you are staying with a friend: (I have plenty of experience hosting and being hosted by friends!)

- Even if people say, 'Make yourself at home,' you should remember that you are not at home (especially if it's a shared house).

- You must be invisible: out of the way during shower time (and your showers should not be longer than 15 minutes!), cooking time and television time. You do not have preference at any time – even if your flatmate is the 'head tenant' in the flat.

- You should respect your friend's schedule: he or she will need to work and do his/her own stuff (cooking, food shopping, etc.)

- You should make sure the house is tidy at all times (especially if your suitcase is in the living room). Do not make a mess by leaving your belongings on the floor EVER! It's very annoying and the flatmates will start hating you and your friend if you do that.

- Be nice to everyone and if you are staying for a week or more, make dinner for them (if they have not asked any money towards the bills, you should be extra nice to them)

- Do not stay at home all day long. Go out, look for a job or if you are just there for a holiday, make sure you are never a nuisance to anyone in the house.

- I would say that 1 week is the MAXIMUM someone should ask as a favour to stay around.

- Last but not least: give a THANK YOU present to your friend and to the house. The flatmates will be very thankful (even a bottle of wine will do!)

Staying with a host family

Host families are normally more mature couples who have a spare room in their house and host international students for a period of time. It is not very common to have young professionals staying with them unless it is for a really short period of time. Younger students (16-18 years old) normally cannot cook or are mature enough to be living alone or with other friends. They stay with a host family where their clothes are washed, their meals are cooked and they have a curfew. Most of their stays last for around a month but you can stay longer, of course.

Some people stay with a host family for 1 or 2 weeks to have a safe place when they arrive in a new country; they can then look for permanent accommodation. Having a local's opinion about location, prices and all the other aspects related to finding accommodation will make things much easier.

I have a cousin named Sileide who works for a Brazilian airline and decided to improve her English skills. She went to Cambridge for a month and studied six hours a day. She stayed with a host family; her host was actually a single lady who had a nice home not far from the school.

Sileide pointed out the advantages and disadvantages to staying with a host family:

Some advantages:

- You are looked after; your meals are cooked and your clothes are washed

- You have your own room (in most cases) and unless you prefer to stay with a friend, you will not be sharing a room with a stranger.

- Normally, the host will be vetted by the agency and will have to provide minimum requirements (such as bed linen, a desk and chair in the room, etc.).

- The house will be well looked after because the hosts live in it.

- You will have the chance to have contact with the culture straight away by conversing and learning the language and the local culture. Obviously, this will be through the eyes of the host so if your host is 60 years old, it will be a completely different experience from a host family in their 30s.

- If they have a son or daughter of your age, he or she may become your friends for life and come to visit you in your country!

Some disadvantages:

- You cannot use the kitchen (in most of the cases)

- Your time is scheduled: 15 minutes for the shower, you have to be at home by 7pm for dinner, etc.

- You cannot bring friends over or have them sleep over.

- You may be living with older people with whom you have nothing in common.

- You may not be able to use the living room.

- You may hate the food that the host prepares (and then realise how great your mum or dad's food actually is!).

Money – Budget!

What's your budget? Here's a simple way to budget for your trip:

Accommodation + Food + Transport + Phone calls = fixed monthly expenses

Accommodation

Depending on where you are going, your budget may not be very realistic. In London, for example, it's totally unrealistic to have £60 (£ = this is the British Pounds symbol) per week for a room. £100 is much more likely to get you a single room in zone 2.

If you are in Sao Paulo (Brazil), where only now people are getting into the culture of sharing, it may be cheaper (around US$200/month for a double room with 3 other people in the flat).

Tokyo is as expensive as London, so be prepared to spend the same if not more in rent.

If the price is shown per week, you need to calculate how much it is per month.

To calculate that, you do the following:

> Price per week x 52 (number of weeks a year) / 12 (months a year).
>
> So, if a room costs €100
> (one hundred euros per week)
>
> 100 x 52 / 12 = €440

This way you can budget precisely how much your room will cost per month.

The reality is: you should not spend more than 40% of your salary in rent; otherwise, it is a bad, very bad deal. Spending more than you can afford will result in your not having much money left at the end of the month for food, transport, fun, etc.

When living on your own (even in a flatshare, you live 'on your own'; your parents are no longer taking care of you), you need to learn to budget the money. This means balancing what you earn minus the on-going bills such as rent, transport, utilities like energy, gas, water, etc. as well as food, going out, having fun and lastly saving – which may not be possible at the beginning.

The sooner you learn to budget, the better. You will realise how much easier life is when you actually plan it. Easier said than done?

When I first moved to London, I had £600 in my pocket and a credit card with a limit of around £200. In my first two years, I managed to travel all over Europe. I had no money saved, but I lived in a shared room (myself and 2 other guys) and I always bought food in cheap supermarkets. When I travelled, I stayed in hostels. In Amsterdam, I had my first experience in a hostel; I was in a room with 13 other people. It was hell: the smell of shoes, the snoring, the farting . . . but I was young so I didn't really care. It was cheap and that's what mattered!

Food

So, if you are wondering how much money you should have for food, my tip is the following:

- Make a list of the food you eat on a weekly basis and find out what supermarket is in the country where you are going and check the prices of food online.

- For example, if you are going to the UK, bananas are £1.00 kilo, milk is £0.80 for a ½ liter, and bread costs £0.90 a loaf.

So this way, you can have a very good idea of how much money you will need each month for groceries.

Transport

For transport costs, do the same calculation you did for a weekly room price (if paid weekly). Can you buy weekly or monthly? Is it cheaper if you buy per month? Do your research to find the monthly cost.

Once you've added extra expenses like pre-paid phone calls, international calls (if you don't have Internet at home – if you do, use Skype or Facebook messenger to talk to your friends and family), you'll have a very good idea of how much money you need during the first months of your trip.

A few days before your trip

The days seem to be going so fast. You don't know where the hours are going. If you are lucky enough to be working (if you have not given up your job), it really helps because your mind is busy with something else.

While you are dealing with all of the practicalities, you will also be dealing with your emotions.

You need to start getting ready to say goodbye to family and friends. There is nothing that anyone can suggest to you about saying goodbye to family and friends; the tears are going to be there . . .

In the airplane during the trip, many thoughts will go through your mind: Am I doing the right thing? Why am I doing this? What's going to happen there?

These questions will be answered day by day. The worry, the doubt and the fear of the unknown will slowly disappear and the excitement, enthusiasm and pride will start growing, as you get closer to your destination.

You can download our app to help you organise your trip abroad and connect with people who are moving to the same country.

Search for 'Moving Abroad' on the App Store.

STAGE 3

Moving

CHAPTER 3

Moving

The day has arrived and you are going to move to another country!

I asked one of my friends:

- ' How do you describe the experience of leaving your country for the first time?'

He answered the following:

- 'The first time you say good bye is the first time you are born again.'

I asked him to explain why and he said:

- 'When you leave your country, the 'old' you stays behind at the airport and the 'new' you boards the plane! Living abroad will expand your views, change your mind, open your eyes to the world and you will never be the same again.'

I understood what he meant. It has happened to me and it will happen to you too. You will grow as a person and have a more critical view about everything simply because you will experience more of the world.

The tears of sorrow when you say good bye – even when you know that you are coming back – are part of this incredible experience you are about to start!

That moment is unique; it's the beginning of a journey that only you will be able to experience.

It's a lifetime experience that you have been planning for a long time.

You will probably cry on the plane. You will ask yourself:

- 'Why am I doing this?'

- 'Is this right?'

- 'Am I going to achieve what I want?'

- 'Am I going to succeed?'

There are so many questions going through your mind but only you will be able to answer them. The answers will come. Just give yourself time!

You are creating your own story and this is what matters at this moment in time.

Once the sorrow of saying goodbye has been overtaken by the excitement of the new experience, it's time to think of how you are going to get to your destination when your airplane lands.

You probably have done research about the place, the city, the town, the country . . . you can't wait to arrive!

After you disembark the plane, go through immigration and passport control and collect your suitcases . . . then the moment arrives!

Your new life begins!

You are scared and excited all at the same time. If you already booked a place to stay, it's just a matter of getting a map and finding the address. If you have booked a hostel/hotel or are staying with a friend, you will have to go through the process of calling, booking appointments and going for viewings. It's a daunting process but you need to go through it (at least once!).

Finding accommodation after you arrive!

Accommodation is the most important part of your journey. Your new home will be your safe harbour, your nest! It is very important you have a comfortable, clean and safe place to live.

If you are already in the country, you have the chance to search for and view flats.

When you are going flat hunting, you need to have in mind (or in hand – written on a notepad, an iPad or phone) the following:

Location / area:

Full address:

Cost per month:

Are bills included? If yes, which ones and, if not, how much are they and which bills you have to share?

Deposit: how much? Is there any government scheme that will protect your deposit?

What furniture is included in the room? What you should bring (duvet, pillow, bed linens)?

Once you've found a few apartments or rooms that you want to view, what do you do?

Make a list or print the ads if you can. It will help to make notes and to remember which ones are the best. There are cities like London, Tokyo or Paris where there are so many people looking for accommodations that sometimes, you need to decide quickly. If you think it's good and you like it (after asking the necessary questions), you should take it.

Numbers, description, size, if it's a shared room, single or double. Here is the description of room options.

- Shared rooms: rooms with two, three or four or even more beds in the same room, so you will be sharing with a friend or strangers.

- Single room: a room with a single bed.

- Double room: a room with a double bed (a bed on which 2 people can easily sleep). You must read the ad properly as you may waste your time (if it's 2 of you) and the room is only for 1 person. Some people don't like living with couples or if the house has a special license, that room may accommodate only one person and so on.

- Twin: a room with 2 single beds

When you call the person who is advertising, you don't need to provide a resume of your life! You may share some information unnecessarily unless you are going to be living with that person. If the room is being advertised by an agency or by a professional landlord, chances are they are too busy to listen to your life story; just get straight to the point. You will be saving charges on your phone bill too.

You will be a bit scared of going on your own to see the place. If this is the case, send an email to a friend or relative to let them know where you are going or send a text to a friend (if you already have one in country where you are living).

Also, book viewings during the day, as some people are really nervous of going to see a room in the evening.

During the viewing, pay attention to the conditions of the house. You probably will not be looking for things like cracks, mould or conditions of the property (later on in this book, you will learn a little bit more about house maintenance), but these things are very important. If the house shows no signs of neglect, the landlord is proactive or even reactive but he does his part.

The main things to look for are:

– Living room: if the flat is fully furnished, does everything belong to the landlord? If the television belongs to one of the tenants and that tenant moves out, you may end up without a TV (which is very annoying) and you don't want to spend money buying one, right?

Look for cobwebs on the ceiling (this will tell you if the house is cleaned regularly).

Are the sofas in good condition?

– Bathrooms: the main issue with bathrooms is mould on the ceiling, mould or rotten silicon around baths and shower cubicles, yellow stains around tiles and rotten wood (around panels or furniture). If you spot any of these issues, you should ask if it's going to be fixed soon.

- Bedroom: test the mattress, the linen and the pillows, if they are provided.

- Sometimes, we don't have an option for certain items, so if you can negotiate with the landlord prior to move in, great! Negotiate everything before signing the contract otherwise you will hear 'it's rented as seen', after you have moved in.

Also be sure that the furniture provided is in good condition. Open the cupboard kitchen doors, fridge, drawers, doors, etc.

I normally check the shower too. In places like Brazil (where the shower is electric), you will not have problems. France and UK have issues with water pressure so make sure you turn the shower on and try it. At one time, I was in Spain for two weeks and rented an apartment on the 3rd floor; the shower was terrible. Because it was so high in the building and was the same system as in the UK, the water pressure was almost non-existent and having a shower was a nightmare. Because I was only there for two weeks, I didn't really care but if you are going to stay in the house for a while, it's worth checking.

The problem is that many people really do not look out for these things and end up in places that look good but do not function properly. Believe me, it will make a huge difference living somewhere that you feel good and can call 'home'!

Contracts

You found a new 'home,' and you are happy because you've found a place to call home. I am sure you will also be worried that you may be getting into a dodgy deal. Before you sign the contract, you need to make sure of a few things.

You should ask for the following information:

- How much is the deposit?

- What is the minimum stay or the length of the contract you are signing?

- How much is the rent per week or per month?

- What is the notice period for you to vacate the room/property)?

- Will you need a guarantor (someone who will pay the rent on your behalf in the event that you cannot pay the rent)?

- Are all bills included? Which ones? Is there a limit to the bills?

Bills: Normally, bills include water, electricity, gas, Internet, TV license (in countries like UK and Germany, you need to purchase a license to watch TV), government tax (this has different names in different countries but all countries have it; it's the tax covering street cleaning, emergency services such as the fire and police departments, etc.).

You also should find out if there is any government body that can help if you have problems with your landlord. Search for a forum or websites that can provide you information if you need help!

Inventory

I almost forgot to mention that you should keep a note of the condition of the room when you move in. This is called 'inventory'.

My friend Carlos moved to Berlin around 1997. It was his first time in Berlin and he was working for a 5 star hotel as an assistant manager. The hotel provided accommodations for the first month until he could find his own place.

He found a beautiful 1 bedroom flat in the centre not far from work. As it was the first time he was renting (he always lived in his own flat), he decided to take pictures of the place as soon as he moved in.

Two years later, he gave notice (because he was going to move to Vienna) and the estate agents agreed on a date for his check out inventory. It was unbelievable what they said.

There was some plasterwork on the ceiling. Because it was a period building, the plasterwork (flowers and angels) looked a bit naff but it was part of the flat, says Carlos.

The story is: the estate agent said that Carlos had placed the decoration in the ceiling and his deposit would not be returned; the landlord would have to remove the plaster work and the deposit would go towards covering the costs.

Luckily, because Carlos still had the pictures and could prove that it was there when he moved in, he received his deposit back.

Lesson learned? So, be sure to make notes and take pictures (and video, if you want) to ensure your deposit will remain intact. You should inform your landlord or your agency within 24 hours (it's normal practise) so you don't get charged.

7 things to do (and not to do) when you move in!

It feels a bit strange to move into a flat or house where you do not know anyone and now you will be sharing your life with them for as long as you live there.

Let's start with introductions. You should be the one being friendly, asking their names, shaking hands, and making small talk. Soon you will find out that you have things in common and the conversation will flow.

The relief that you feel after you've moved in is immense. You are now relaxed and you can start doing your 'things' again - painting your nails every Monday, watching rugby on YouTube, cooking your spaghetti Bolognese for lunch, etc.

Your daily routine is coming back and you start to enjoy your new environment. It's not just because the place you chose is comfortable and your flatmates seem to be very friendly; it's because now you can have your life back to normal – in some ways.

I remember how happy a Spanish flatmate of mine was when she moved into our house in Marylebone (North London); we had a huge kitchen and she could have her 'jamon'. It wasn't until I spent a week in Spain that I realised how happy she was when she brought home the entire leg of a pig. She was thrilled because it was the first time she was in a house where there was enough space to have that in the kitchen and her flatmates would not be upset. So she could enjoy her jamon in peace, even though she was not in Spain. You see the things that make people happy because they have a good home?

So, during your first week in the flat and your first two or three weeks in the new country, you have already managed to make friends, you have a home and you (may) have a job.

7 things you should do when you move into a new flat

1 - Show that you know something about their country.

You should show some knowledge about their country. People feel proud when you say things about their country. So, making sure that you have something nice about their country is a good way to become friends with your new flatmates. If you do not know anything about their country, do not say anything. Do your research and next time, show that you actually 'know something.'

Also, be the best advocate for your own country. People will take your views and opinions about your own country so if you say nice things and teach people what is great about your culture, others will take your word for it. So, be sure you make your brothers and sisters proud!

2 – Cook for them once in a while.

Everyone loves being pampered every now and again and flatties are no different.

At one time, I lived in East Dulwich (South London) and it was a great house. Everyone cooked for each other. The atmosphere was amazing. So if you really want to get to know them and show consideration towards them, make a nice dinner! People will be happy together and the conversation will flow. It will completely break the ice and get everyone talking.

3 – Invite them to join you for a drink.

Being in a different environment will do wonders for your new friendship. Whatever drink you decide to have with your flatmates – alcoholic or not – the friendship will develop from there.

Being away from the house will lead to different conversations and you will soon find out if you have things in common or not.

4 - Ask about the house rules (if there are any).

Once introductions are out of the way, it's time to get on with the house rules. No one does that and it seems so obvious to me.

Ask people in the house if there are house rules that you should be aware of.

What time do people have showers in the morning? What are their cooking habits? Friends over during the week? Parties? TV time . . .

There are so many stories of people who ended up arguing over small things or everyday tasks.

Flatsharing is like a marriage without sex! You have to cook together, live together and end up developing feelings for each other but you don't sleep with your flatmates.

Don't be shy to ask about the rules. It will show that you have consideration and are eager to learn so you get along with everyone.

5 - Make sure you understand the idiomatic expressions.

Something else that no one tells you is that you will misunderstand things and those misunderstandings can kill friendships.

I have a story about a text message that I received and I didn't know the expression: 'good for you.'

The English have this expression; when you achieve something or when you do something good they say 'good for you!' meaning that they are congratulating you for your accomplishment. In Brazil, there is a similar expression but it's ironic so depending on how you say it, it can mean completely the opposite and that you are in a way demeaning that action.

I had a friend whom I liked very much and I had just got my first job in London and texted her. She texted me back, saying 'good for you'. Because I didn't know the expression in English, I took it the wrong way and thought she was jealous that I had gotten a job and she didn't. I didn't text her back after that. After about a week, she texted me again, asking if everything was fine and why I didn't reply to her messages?

After about a month, I was still upset with her; we bumped into each other on the street and she asked why I hadn't returned her calls or text messages. I told her in a very angry way how upset I was with her jealousy and then I mentioned the text message. She laughed at me and explained what she really had meant.

That was another lesson learnt. After that, I always asked people twice to explain what they really meant before I got annoyed again. So, if you are new to the country (wherever you are) and learning the language, you need to know there will be expressions that are similar to those in your language but mean something completely different.

I suppose if you are reading this book, you will never get to this stage because you are going to be aware before someone says something - but if it does happen, ask for an explanation so you don't get upset for nothing!

This can also happen when you are in a relationship with someone but we will talk about relationships later on.

6 – Do clean up after yourself.

There is nothing more annoying than having to use the toilet, the bathroom sink or the bath after a flatmate who has not cleaned it properly.

Sounds like common sense? Yes, it does but it seems that not everyone gets the idea.

The most disgusting thing is to go for a shower (if the shower is above the bath) and there is hair all over it.

Friendship has boundaries and they should not be crossed. Respect is everything.

If you brush your teeth, make sure you rinse the toothpaste from the sink. You would not like to find the sink dirty, right? So why would you do it then?

The same applies for the dishes. The dishes are actually the number one issue in flatshares.

I will talk more about the dishes later on.

7 – Give your flatmates space.

As much as you love talking to your flatmates and like being friendly, people sometimes just want their own peace, to be in silence, quiet in their own world.

They want to watch TV and not be disturbed. They want to pay attention to the documentary; they are not interested in your auntie's love affair at that moment.

You need to learn that, so you can get along with them even better. As much as being friendly and talkative is a cool thing to do, giving them space and time for themselves – even if you are in the same room – makes life even more harmonious for everyone.

7 Things you should not do after moving in to a new flat

1 - Don't generalise.

People tend to generalise a lot when they meet one or two people from a country; when they talk about the citizens of that country, they make comments that 'Brazilians are like this', 'Germans are like that', 'the French bla bla bla . . . '

Of course, you cannot generalise a whole nation because you meet someone who has that habit or behaves in a certain way. There are peculiar people in every nation (no, I am not generalizing; it's a fact!! – lol.)

There is nothing worse than meeting someone and the person saying: 'Oh, you are German! Do you lie around naked whenever you can?' How do you think that person is going to react? He or she will dislike you immediately. I know for a fact because I worked with a German guy and during his first week in London, he told me that story and said: 'French people are very rude, they have no manners and have no social skills.'

So, you understand my point here? One comment leads to another and the dislike starts so he will be talking to his friends about how rude the French are because of that one comment. It maybe was a 'joke' but sometimes jokes can be interpreted in very different ways.

2 - Do not eat their food.

One thing you must NOT do is to take your flatmate's food from the fridge or cupboard when they have not given permission! Normally, people will not talk about it but it happens very often. Be up front; send a text message or ask straight away. Trying to hide that you ate your flatmate's last two slices of bread because you didn't have any and you were in a rush to go to work will just create problems and will involve the other people if it's not only the two of you sharing the flat.

Stealing food from people may lead to people ganging up against you and you will end up isolated. The last thing you want is to feel lonely at home. It is the worst feeling ever and it will make your life really miserable.

3 - Do not 'share' their items (beauty products, perfume, washing powder . . .).

I upset a flatmate once because I used one of his disposable razors and didn't say anything. I was about 26 at the time, I was in a rush for a date and didn't have any more razors. He had a bag with ten so I decided to use one. He didn't say anything so a few weeks later, I used another one.

One day we were having dinner and he mentioned that I was very immature and he was not happy that I was doing that.

He then decided to move out. I thought it was a bit harsh but I understand him now. It's annoying. It's theft. If you take something from someone without his or her knowledge, you are stealing what is theirs and nobody likes to have their things being stolen, right?

Think about that next time you are about to do it!

4 – Do not leave paper messages everywhere.

Only now I understand how much my former Colombian flatmates must have hated me. I used to do that a lot. There is nothing more annoying that a Posit on the fridge saying 'drink your own f***ing milk, you idiot!'.

I have to say that it's very childish and annoying.

At one time, I lived with some Australians and they did that to me. It used to drive me crazy. Why don't people simply say something? I suppose if there are a lot of people in the house, it's easier to be anonymous so they avoid confrontation. It just makes things worse, believe me!

5 – Do not have parties during work days (Monday to Friday).

Unless you are all the same age, have the same jobs and the same lifestyle (i.e., all students or all unemployed!), you should not have parties on weekdays or invite people over for drinks after around 11pm. This is so annoying. I lived with four guys once and a Belgium flatmate (unemployed) used to bring his friends on Tuesdays and Wednesdays for drinks. I didn't mind so much at the beginning but they stayed later and later until around 3am.

I had to wake up at 8am the following day, so having people laughing, listening to music, etc. until all hours was not the best situation.

Even after I asked them nicely to stop, they would continue with the giggling until one day I lost my temper and asked everyone to leave. I literally opened the door and kicked everyone out of the flat.

Crazy? Maybe it was a bit over the top but I never had to do that again. They never came back during the week. The Belgium flatmate and I never exchanged a word again and three weeks later, he went back to Belgium because he could not find a job in London.

So, make sure you respect people who work during the week . . . not only your flatties but also the neighbours.

6 – Do not have your boyfriend or girlfriend overstaying.

If for whatever reason, people do not want partners staying over, you should respect that.

Some people say that living with couples changes the dynamics in the flat. I agree with that to a certain extent. If you have a new person in your life, make sure you share the 'staying over' between your flat and theirs. Ask your flatmates what is acceptable for them. Two nights, three nights?

I suppose you must be thinking: 'I pay rent, it's my place too' but you are paying rent for yourself and the others are living with you, not with two people! If you respect that, you guys are going to live in a much harmonious place!

7 – Don't leave your stuff around the common areas.

Some flatmates think that the living room and corridors are extensions of their bedrooms! They are not! Do not leave your stuff around the house as if you live on your own!

If you live with a tidy-freak person, it will drive them mad and you will certainly generate conflict.

You collection of DVDs is a very cool thing to have but make sure you keep it in your bedroom, on a shelf, so your flatmates do not have to tidy the living room every time they want to watch TV!

The big monster!!!

Landlords, owners, proprietors and whatever else you decide to call them!

If you think that dealing with your parents or your siblings was difficult, you have never dealt with landlords. That's what owners of properties are called in the UK. In France and Brazil, they are called proprietors and in different countries, they will have different names. Whatever they are called, they are the ones who have the last say on how and what happens to the house when it comes to spending money on it. Some of them are actually nice and reasonable. Some of them are not so reasonable and they are almost impossible to contact.

Love them or hate them, you need them. They own the properties where you (and your friends) will be living, so you may as well develop a good relationship with them.

It is difficult to give you tips on how to deal with them

because their interest in the property is going to be different from yours so you never know if you are going to be able to deal with them amicably or not.

I remember I had a Lebanese landlord who always made a huge fuss when we complained that something was broken. I believe he thought that if he shouted at us often enough, we would not bother him anymore but that didn't really work with us. We ended up moving out because we found him to be very unreasonable.

The reality is: things will stop working at some point. They will break, block, or get damaged.

To a certain extent, you (as the tenant) will be liable for payment but sometimes, the landlord will have to pay for it.

For example: if you are washing your clothes and you forget coins in the pocket of your trousers. The coins may damage the washing machine. The coins will probably get stuck in the filter and the washing machine will stop. Who pays for this?

YOU, of course.

If the washing machine is old and it stops working (i.e., never spins again), the landlord has to either fix it or replace it.

I have a lot of funny stories involving landlords. Here are some of them:

Landlord and inspections

Sometimes landlords like doing inspections in the properties to make sure you are not growing cannabis in the house or have a dead body in your wardrobe.

During one of these inspections, our African flatmate was caught naked, taking picture for a sex website. So, if someone knocks at your door, you should say – DO NOT ENTER because if you remain silent – like our flattie did – you may end up naked in front of your landlord!

In the closet!

I will never forget when I lived in Kennington and I had a flatmate from Poland called Marek. During the few months after he moved in, his girlfriend was constantly in the house and she was not the friendliest person. It was part of our contract that we could not have a partner living with us; we knew she was there with him one day so we called the landlord straight away. The landlord came and asked to do an inspection of the house. We were fully aware that she was in his room so when the landlord asked to check his room, we said that would be fine.

The first thing the landlord did was to open the wardrobe door and there she was. Marek had hidden her inside the closet. A few days later he moved out and I never heard from Marek again.

When you find out the mortgage is not being paid

Sometimes, landlords get into a difficult financial situation and stop paying their mortgage (mortgage is when you borrow money from the bank to buy a house).

When there were letters to 'The Occupier,' we opened them; the letters stated the house would be repossessed (the bank would take them from the owner) by the bailiffs.[1] We found out the house was going to auction because the mortgage had not been paid for over six months, even though the rent we were paying more than covered the mortgage on a monthly basis. It was very stressful and we had to find another place before the bank changed the locks and we were unable to get back in.

Leaks and repairs

I had a really good Polish friend back in 2004 who lived in North London; every now and again, I would visit her. Her house was so badly maintained that she had mushrooms growing under her bath. I remember taking pictures with her and sending to the landlord. His response? 'Are you growing magic mushrooms in the flat? I will terminate your contract if you do!'

We laughed at first but when we realised that the landlord was actually serious and was trying to blame my friend for the mushrooms, we contacted the authorities to deal with it!

Mickey Mouse

I know it sounds funny to talk about Mickey Mouse but having one or seven living with you is not fun. When I lived alone in a studio in East London, I remember being woken up by a mouse eating my carrots. I don't

---

1 Bailiffs - A person who performs certain actions under legal authority. So if you don't pay your rent, the landlord can contact the court and bailiffs will be sent to the house to remove you.

know how the mouse managed to get on top of my dining table where I had a bowl of fruit and vegetables. I was shocked to see Mickey Mouse there and had no alternative but get the broom and hit him. Several times, I was woken up by mice in the house. It is hard to point out who is to blame or to pay for the infestation when there is an issue like this. That's why you need to make sure your contract clearly states all the points – including pest infestation. In the end, I just moved out because I could not bear the idea of living with so many of them. However, you should not have to move out. Your landlord should deal with the situation if it's an infestation in the house.

Moving out and leaving things behind

The most annoying things is moving from a property and forgetting something in the cupboard or fridge, etc. Normally, landlords will charge you to remove them. Their 'time' is very expensive, so make sure the house is cleaned throughout before you leave.

Private items around the house

One of my workmates once told me how embarrassing the situation was when the landlord decided to go to his house for an inspection.

He was living with two lesbians and on a Tuesday afternoon, there was going to be an inspection from the local authority to check the state of the property and the landlord would be present. They requested someone that lived in the house also to be there to answer questions that might come up.

The embarrassing situation was that the lesbians didn't get along well with one of the flatmates and they left a dildo in the bath on purpose.

My workmate said that it was the funniest and most embarrassing situation he ever experienced. The landlord looked at the council officer and they all laughed.

So, if anyone is coming to your house for an inspection, please make sure you remove everything from the common areas and hide things under you bed – at least the things that should not be seen!

Burglary

During my time as a tenant and as a landlord, I have been the victim of robbery. But whose fault is it if there is a robbery? Well, this will all depend of the circumstances. In Vauxhall, South London, I was going to do a viewing in a house. I was about to reach the property when I saw a young man running from the house with a suitcase. I then learned that he had stolen all the laptops, cameras and iPods of everyone in the house it was a 5-bedroom house with 6 people living in it.

Whose fault was it? The tenants left the window open and the thief came through it, unfortunately.

What is maintenance?

Now, back to your new flat and everyday life – including the maintenance!

You are settled in and you know where you are going to study or work. You know where the supermarket is, you translated a list of food so you can go shopping and things are going perfectly well.

The only issue is when something goes wrong. You never thought a wardrobe door would actually 'stop working' until now, did you? Well, the reality is that things need maintenance.

Even your body needs maintenance!

You need to cut your nails every 4 weeks or so, you need to cut your hair, you have to use moisturiser to delay the process of getting old . . . all this is 'body maintenance'!

Flats or houses or apartments or whatever you call your 'home' needs maintenance too!

The hinges, the wheels, the handles . . . basically everything that is used every day needs to be 'maintained' and you can do it too!

I am not going to teach you how to build a house but there are things that you can do to make sure everything is working fine. A screwdriver, a hammer and/or a few tools can prolong the life of many items!

Fix before it breaks!

If you are a girl reading this book and have tons of clothes, chances are your wardrobe will be damaged by the amount of stuff you are trying to push into it!

Sometimes, having three or four tops or jackets on one hanger will push the wardrobe door and the number of times that you change your clothes also means that door will be opened and closed 1000 more than the wardrobe of your male flatmates! This is a FACT, not a theory that I created!!!

This means that your door is much more likely to start showing signs of use or what is called 'wear and tear' (basically, you use something so much that will tear at some point).

If it starts to get wobbly, get a screwdriver; if you don't have one, a knife will do. Just tighten the screws and the door will last a few more months until the 100000th time you open and close and it's time to tighten it again!

The same may happen to the handles of drawers, wardrobes and everything else that opens and closes and needs a screw or nails to hold in place!

So if you see something getting loose, wobbly or going somewhere that it shouldn't, you must pay attention before it breaks completely!

That's why I always say: 'fix it before it breaks,' Otherwise, it is too late and your landlord will end up charging you for a new item – especially if you do not say anything about it!

The bathroom!

Ahhhh, the bathroom!

This is the place where people do their bits! All sorts of bits!

They shave, they trim, they cut, they dry, they blow dry, they blow . . . let's not go there! I will tell you about flatmates and relationships later on.

The bathroom is the room in the flat that will 'suffer' more than any other! The toilet will be blocked, the bath plug will be blocked, the sink plug will be blocked and so on and so on . . .

What do you do if you block any of these things?

Buy caustic soda. That's the first recommendation. It really melts clumps of long hair and anything else.

Landlords hate bathrooms. If they could rent a flat without a bathroom, they would! They are the reason landlords hate being landlords!

Plumbers love bathrooms; yes, they do! Because they make a lot of money, especially when that young guy who loves bringing girls home on the weekend blocks the toilet with condoms . . .

During the time that I have managed flats, there have been so many reports with 'foreign objects' that at some point, we decided to place notes by the toilets. Not post it notes but nice, polite, laminated, laminated ones (professional looking!)

The kitchen!

It's where the party always is, isn't it?

People love being in the kitchen; it's the heart of the house. The food, the cooking together . . . the dishes! AH! The dishes!

So many people have argued over the dishes but not only that, they have hated each other because of the leftovers people leave in the sink after they do the dishes. Be careful with food down the sink. It will block the pipes and your landlord will charge you to unblock it. Again, caustic soda will help, or try Mr. Muscle!

I remember when we had an Italian girl living in the house and everybody started hating her. Slowly, she was being ignored and becoming isolated. She always left her pasta plugging the sink and after calling the landlord twice, he said he would charge us because it was our fault that the sink was always blocked.

The third time he sent the plumber, there was so much spaghetti in the pipe that she had to pay for the plumber callout. In London, this service is quite expensive so she learned her lesson. It was probably the most expensive pasta she ever ate!

Sharing the fridge is another issue. People think because they share a flat, they can share the bread, the milk, everything. Listen to my advice! Stay away from other people's food! (Remember the 7 DO's and 7 DON'T's ?)

I know; sometimes you just need a glass of milk or two eggs for the cake you are making, but unless you ACTUALLY replace it, it will create problems between you and your flatmate(s).

Living room

This is where you gossip, chat, share life, cry and so many other things. In the UK, people also call it the sitting room, parlour, lounge or drawing room.

The living room is a place to relax, but make sure you

do not make it an extension of your bedroom by leaving your stuff all around!

Looking after yourself

Building confidence

One thing that you will realise is that you will feel slightly afraid and you will lose your confidence when you first go abroad. Because you do not know anything about the place, you don't know where the streets are, the locations of certain stores and you may not know anyone around, you feel scared and worried.

If you are going to a country where the language is completely different, you seem to wait longer to have your 'voice heard'. You listen much more than you speak and this may not even be the way you are normally but because of the circumstances, you need to adapt.

My younger sister is going through this process at the moment. She has left Brazil (for the second time) and is in England learning English to be able to get a better job in Brazil. This is something that many young professionals do. They plan to develop themselves in their careers and they end up developing themselves as people.

It's very hard to explain how it works but if you are reading this book, you have already started this process.

You will be in situations that you wouldn't be in if you were in your own country and you need to be able to go through them by yourself.

My sister was telling me the other day that even the simplest things become a personal challenge and even though I was a phone call away, she needed to make sure she could do things on her own so she would learn. This is about growing up and becoming mature. You will no longer have your parents to back you up; you cannot run to them if something goes wrong. The only thing they can do now is listen to you or see you via Skype. You will probably listen to their advice (or not) but at the end of the day, you will make your own decisions.

This is what is going to make you stronger. The more simple, everyday decisions you make, the more you will feel confident and empowered. It's a great feeling to know that you are achieving what you want.

A Thai friend of mine once said: 'I have no idea why I am in London at the moment but this is the reason I am here. At some point, I will find myself. I am only 21 and I don't know what I like or want as a career. Meeting people, working in different places and doing different jobs that I would not normally do in my country will help me to clear my mind'.

I always thought that was very mature of him. He was only 21 and he had no idea what he wanted. His journey in London was actually to find what he loved in life.

This is completely different from my younger sister, you see. She knows what she wants and she is here to reach a goal. So when I said that people normally would have a similar story, now you understand why. They both have a goal. They are completely different, but the journey to reach that goal is very similar.

Feeling homesick

After you started feeling more 'at home', you will be constantly be looking on Facebook and be in touch with your friends back in your home country; you will be calling your parents and probably your best friend too. Now that life is getting back to 'normal', you can start thinking about them again. All the work in finding the new place is paid off.

When you have more time on your hands to think about your life, you will start feeling sad. You will be missing your friends and family so much that you think you cannot complete the journey.

It has been around 3 months now since you moved away and now you think: what is this about?

You will start feeling homesick. If I were in front of you now, you would be asking me 'what is homesick', right?

There are different ways to explain:

The Wikipedia definition of homesick is: a feeling of longing for one's familiar surroundings.

The website dictionary.com definition is: sad or depressed from a longing for home or family while away from them for a long time.

Basically, homesick is when you are missing family, friends and familiar places, belongings and routines that you had when you were in your country.

Everyone feels this at some point. It comes and goes. There are moments that I still feel homesick, even after 11 years aways from Brazil.

What do you do to stop feeling homesick?

Well, everyone is different and the way you deal with it will be different too.

How to stop feeling homesick

- *Remind yourself why you have moved to another country* The first thing that you must remind yourself is why you are there. What's the goal to be achieved? New language, new career, new life in general? If you are not sure, read Chapter 1 again.

- *How long will you be away?* Is your move temporary? How so? 3 months, 1 year, until the end of your degree?

  This will help you to keep your mind on your goal. If you don't know why you are travelling and you just want to run away from all your problems, then things are a little bit more complicated . . .

- *What are you missing?* What are you missing the most? Material things you can get online (your favourite biscuit, the brand of body cream that ONLY can be found in your country, etc.).

- *Friends and family* If you are missing your friends and family there are a few things you can do. Skype and   Facebook are two of the best ways you can keep in touch. Seeing them will help you to be 'closer.' I know it's not the same but unless you take a plane and fly back home, you will have to make-do with the tools you have to stop feeling homesick.

- *Make friends with people from your own country*
One way to keep your homesickness under
control is to make friends with people from
your   country. In your first months away, you
will probably meet a lot of people from your
country   and that's a good thing. If
they have been living there for a long time, it
will be quicker and   easier for you to learn
about the habits, how things operate in the
city and the places to go   (and not to go!).

Being   friends   with   people   from   your
country will have advantages and as well as
disadvantages. You need to understand that
if you do not mix with locals (whatever they
may be ... English, Argentinean, South African
and so on), you will not learn about them.
You need to live 'their life', go to their houses,
to their parties, and have dinner with them.

You need to experience what it is to be like them;
otherwise, what is the point of moving abroad
only to mix with people from your country?

You may as well stay at home and do a course
around the corner from your house, right?

Health

The first three months are the crucial ones, not only
about how you feel – your mind going crazy about
everything and all the information that you need to
process at the same time – but also about your health.

Your body needs to adapt to the new climate. If you are

from a hot country and move to a cold one, your body will be in shock. Be prepared 'to be sick' so that's when your medication comes in handy (if you took any with you).

Remember what I mentioned in Chapter 1 about what you will need before you leave your country? If you don't remember, go back and check the items.

It's time to use them!

Of course, it's not set in stone. Some people are stronger than others but if you are like most people, your body will have a reaction, especially if the climate is very different, and you will need to look after yourself more. You must be very careful at work too. Remember the first three months are crucial in any job, so if you are sick too often during that time, it will send a bad signal to your employer and they may not consider extending your contract.

The food that you will eat will also help. Eating nutritious food will help your immune system to stay strong. Translating the name of food from your language into the language of the country where you are will help a lot You soon will learn that chicken, cow, pork and fish are sold everywhere in the world; all that is different are the ways they are prepared. That's all.

Weather

If you are moving somewhere that is very different from your own country, i.e., if you are from Brazil and moving to the UK or if you are Italian moving to New York, the weather will have a huge impact in your life. You need to be prepared for it.

If it rains a lot, if it's colder than you are used to, if it's hotter and so on.

Do your research to make sure you will be able to cope (and how to cope) with the weather where you are going. If it's too hot, you have to consider sunblock (at all times); if it's too cold, you need to wear clothes that will keep you warm. Just to let you know that clothes make a big difference.

When I left Brazil and went to France, it was in the middle of December. December is very hot in Sao Paulo, an average of 38C, while in France, it averages 4C so it's a shocking temperature change. It's like going from an oven directly into a freezer. My winter clothes from Brazil could not stop the cold simply because 'cold' in Brazil is 15C, so we do not need super heavy jackets – like we do in Europe.

When I first moved to the UK, I wore long johns. They are like tights for men (but they are not actually tight) and keep you very warm.

You have no idea how much the weather and your health can have an effect on you.

If you are healthy and do not have issues with being too cold or too hot, you will be happy and your trip will be much more pleasurable.

Dealing with culture shock

Culture shock is sometimes the main reason why some people cannot survive a trip abroad.

The differences between cultures can be so shocking that they cannot adapt, accept or understand the differences (or do not want to) and end up going back home early.

Just so you understand what I am talking about, I will tell you the story of a Chinese girlfriend of mine who has been living in London for over 20 years. Her name is Lucy and she moved to London when she was 20 years old.

We met when we were both studying French and we became friends on the second day of our course. We were doing the course because both of us had French partners.

Lucy is an adorable woman. I learnt to like her as it was a bit difficult to get under her skin at the beginning of our friendship. She is sweet, thoughtful and practical.

Lucy is from Hong Kong and people from Hong Kong make it very clear they are not from mainland China – it seems that Hong Kong Chinese are a special breed.

During the several hundred hours of conversations we've had so far, I learnt so much about Asians. Do you remember what I told you about being the ambassador of your country?

I think Lucy has done that very well. The way I see her country is a direct reflection of how I interact with her. She is very thoughtful, practical and she can control her emotions very well. Apparently, these are skills common to Asians and they can keep things under control very well.

She explained to me that they normally do not like

sharing accommodation. It's very rare to see Chinese people sharing with other nationalities. They normally like sticking together. I asked her once if this is because the culture is so different.

She replied: 'Most probably yes. I cannot answer in name of everyone in China (as there are quite a few of us!) but sharing is not something we are used to. We do not leave our parents' home early like Europeans do. We stay around with our families instead of going to live with strangers. Flats in China are all very small; there are no 4, 5 or 6 bedrooms (unless you are very rich) and there is no flatshare culture. We also have different cooking habits and we work a lot. We are used to there being quite a few of us in the same house.

I believe the culture is changing a bit now but the Chinese do not trust other cultures. Because they have a way of thinking, they think only if you think the same way it would work'.

We talked about her experience when she moved to the UK from Hong Kong and it was slightly different from the normal student who would come for a few years and then come back.

Lucy arrived in the UK because her company was moving. She was looked after and didn't have the worries that one has when moves to another country. She said she was looking forward to moving abroad. She wanted to meet people, learn different things and see the world with her own eyes.

When we talked about her first experience with sharing a flat, she started laughing.

'I tell you why I am laughing – she said – I moved in

with a Jewish lady who was 89!'

She continued her story with a smile on her face – 'It was my first time abroad and I wanted to find a house myself. I saw an ad from an agency and went there to see what they had available. I thought it was a good opportunity to start. It was a nice house in Swiss Cottage, a relatively rich area of North London. The lady was probably looking for company rather than money for the room. Age does not mean anything; she was pleasant and played tennis twice a week. Also, she went to the market and cooked her lunch every day. She was very active. Although we didn't have anything in common, I enjoyed living there. I could bring a friend – I had to ask permission – but I was not allowed to have male guests overnight!' Lucy laughed hysterically at this point in the conversation.

The conversation continues.

'It is not that I wanted to but I was 20 and I no longer lived with my parents. There were advantages as well; I never had issues with the dishes, she was very quiet, I had the whole house to myself sometimes and the kitchen was amazing!

I had to move out after she passed away. It was very sad. I moved to Wapping and lived with BBC (British born Chinese) - I didn't know they had a code for that - but I didn't live there long.

The mentality was very different. Even though we were all Chinese in the house, I never really socialised with them. We were friendly towards each other but I felt there was nothing in common. Because of that, I isolated myself from them and it was not a joyful experience.

After 6 months I gave notice and moved out. I was socialising a lot with people from work. I had contact with them before (when the head office was in Hong Kong) so it was like I knew them.

One of my work colleagues was looking for a lodger and I moved into their spare room. It was my first contact with gay men, as well as all the other experiences I had.

In Hong Kong, I had never met anyone who was gay. There was no pre-concept, because you can't have pre-concept of something you do not know exists!' - she said, almost explaining herself.

'It was the best decision of my life! They were an amazing couple. They made me feel really welcomed and I felt I was finally learning the English culture – as I was living with English people and seeing their everyday life, the language, learning what they cooked and enjoying their dinner parties. The English love their dinner parties and to show off their cooking skills - even though their cuisine is not the most exotic and diversified.

We had a family relationship. They were extremely caring and we never, ever haYou see, until you actually experience living with people in their own country, you cannot really have an opinion about them. You can never generalise but some habits are influenced by the culture you are brought up in.

7 ways to deal with cultural shock:

1 - Sightsee first.

You will probably have lots to worry about before you can relax in your new city, but being a tourist and sightseeing to know the city well is the first step in getting to know your whereabouts.

Do all the cheesy things, take pictures, be silly, and make funny faces as if you would not go back there. You need to be sure to do that in the beginning because the novelty will wear off after a while; soon, you'll have a routine and not much time to be walking around taking pictures.

Get a map, local guides and click click click away your best shots!

2 - Make friends with both the locals (at least 1!) and with someone from your own country.

This could be the first step to becoming a real friend of the 'culture.' You will need to understand them, see how they live. Ask lots of questions. Soon you will see that people feel really proud about where they are from. You normally see how proud they are if you criticise. They are allowed to criticise their country, but you are not!

Also, you make people feel special when you show interest in them. Your new friend will be the guide, the 'Google answer' for the questions you are going to have. There is no Google in the world that compares to talking to a local about their culture.

Andiara (my younger sister) says that it is much easier when you arrive in a new country to make friends, especially if you meet people from the same country who arrived at the same time. You sympathise with them, have the same doubts, shocks and you ask yourselves the same questions. You will have many hours of conversation. Just make sure you don't go criticising everything about the country.

I particularly dislike when I meet people in London and they say 'I hate English food, I hate English weather . . .' My answer to that is always the same: 'go back to your country if it's so much better there!'

It sounds harsh but no one likes to hear criticism, right?

Especially if it's about the country where you have chosen to live – whatever that country is!

3 – Go for walks and coffees.

Very soon, you learn the habit of the locals (especially if you make a local friend) and the best way to develop this friendship is going for walks. Not only you will see your local area (or any area you decide to walk around), but also the conversation flows better. You will learn about the city, as well as the culture.

Meeting people for a coffee seems to be an international cultural exchange. People loving meeting to chat about life, to gossip and catch up!

I remember once having a chat with a friend in a Vietnamese Cafe in London where they serve this piping hot coffee with condensed milk, which was divine. Then, my friend told me she was pregnant. The place was marked by the occasion and the coffee with condensed milk has been on top of my list ever since!

4 – Talk positively about things.

During your coffee catch-up with your friend, make sure you discuss nice things about their culture.

I love the English rules of ceremony, for example. The English seem to have a whole etiquette about how to run a ceremony and they are very good at it. Brazilians transform everything in a party and gosh, Brazilians can party!

You see, there is always something good about a culture. Indians have wonderful food (and no, it isn't all spicy, as I learnt).

The more you learn about the new culture, the easier is for you to like it.

5 – Face up to everyday challenges.

Eleanor Roosevelt was famous for saying that you should do something that takes courage every day. When you first move to a new country, everything takes three times as long to be completed. Even when you have to go to the supermarket to buy your own food!

Buying your metro ticket for the first time will take a long time, especially if you don't know if it's daily, weekly, discount if you are student, discount if you are under 26 years old, etc., etc.

That's why doing your research online will cut this

time in half, although you can learn about them online but when it gets to the machine, you still need to learn how to operate it.

Just make sure that you see everything as an adventure, not as a chore! You will have much more fun and feel better if you see it this way!

6 – Keeping some of your routines and something special from your home country.

Once you learnt the name of your favourite food, make sure you cook it as often as you like. For example, I love pudim (the Brazilian desert that I mentioned earlier on) and it was only after about 3 years I decided to learn to make it, which made me feel more at home. When friends come for dinner, that's what I serve!

A friend of mine loves watching Brazilian soap operas, so YouTube and other streaming websites help him to 'feel at home'.

I believe that the best thing to make you feel good about your country is music! There is nothing like listening to your favourite singer. You close your eyes and you are back home!

You have no idea how special if feels when you ask someone to bring your favourite little things that you cannot find anywhere. Depending which city you move to, you may not find your favourite biscuits, shampoo, hair removal cream, etc.

Ask someone to send the things you miss the most via a friend or by the post. It makes you feel so good inside. It's a weird, childish sensation but it's great.

7 – Keep a diary or a journal (written or pictures).

When you first arrive, you should try to keep a diary of some sort in which to keep your story.

These days, people write blogs; they film themselves or take pictures and put them on Facebook. These are ways to keep the memory fresh.

One of my friends created an album for every year and chose one picture for every month to represent his life that month. It was really cool.

Another friend of mine made a blog for the first three months, stopped for three months and then wrote again for three months. We laughed at the situations he was in when he first arrived. You see, there are so many ways to keep the story going. You just need to find your own way to record your story, especially if you have a time frame, like one year or two years and then going back home.

STAGE 4

The upgrade

CHAPTER 4
THE UPGRADE

You may not really be aware when Stage 4 starts. It may be after you've been living abroad for a year, it may be two . . .

In my case, it started three years after I moved to London.

This stage is when you feel more 'at home' and you want your life to be better. You want to 'upgrade' your home. You want to live with fewer people. You want to live in a nicer house; you want to live in a nicer area. You may be dating someone and have plans to be live together.

Your friendships are now more solid and deeper so you are more selective with the people you talk to and become friends with.

There is no need to talk to everyone and try to be friends with everyone you meet any more, like you used to do when you first arrived in the country. You've probably mastered the language quite well.

Now, let's explore this stage a bit more. This is the stage of developing deeper roots in the country. It is the stage of getting a better job, moving up the social 'ladder'. You earn more money and you go to more expensive bars. You want intellectually challenging conversations. You prefer nicer restaurants – slightly more expensive than the Chinese take-aways you ate when you first arrived.

It's a natural process that will happen to you – it happens to everyone!

You will lose some friends along the way. This is also normal. If you decide that you want to improve yourself and your life, some of your friends may not follow you. They are happy with their lives; they do not see why you need to get a better job or even get out of your comfort zone.

Slowly, you lose contact with some people and you don't understand why. But I do.

I call it *natural selection*. It means that you are starting a new stage; therefore, you need new people, new challenges, new conversations, for the 'new you.' People that will be in the same level: intellectually, financially, socially or whatever level you feel that people should be so you can be relate to them.

It's not just that. Your tastes will change. If you have been hanging out with people who love going to clubs to listen to house music, you may now prefer something not so loud, a little bit classier, where you can talk, enjoy the conversation and the company.

This is the upgrade stage of your life. You will go through the upgrade several times in life. As you get older, you upgrade everything. Every stage of your life has an upgrade that you are going to deal with. Believe me! I am going through one at the moment and it is not the first time.

You may be in one at the moment, and you were not aware!

Time to choose who YOU want to live with

Choosing a flatmate

After you have been living in the same house for a while and one of your flatmates decides to move out, it's time to choose who you want to share with. If you are in a house where you can choose the flatmate, you will have to go through the process of interviewing flatmates. My advice to you is to ask some of the questions below. If you do not want to ask them directly, make sure you lead the conversation into the subject you want to find out about.

It's pretty much like a lottery because you never know what the person is going to be like when living with them.

There are a few basic questions you can ask them.

About money:

- What is your job?

This normally is the first question they ask. Also, you need to find out if the future flatmate will be coming home late and how late. Nurses, for example, work different shifts so they may arrive late at night. If you have wood flooring, the noise can be an issue as well as the noise that showers make, especially when is complete silence in the flat late at night.

- If the bills are shared

If you have to share the bills, do not be embarrassed to ask if they pay their bills on time.

Tell them that if they fail to pay the bills on time three times, they will be asked to leave. Do not be afraid to say things upfront. The clearer you are about the rules, the easier it will be to avoid problems living together.

About habits:

- Do you smoke?

If you do not smoke and if this is an issue for you make it very clear that he or she will not be able to smoke at all in the flat or only in the garden.

You should read your contract as well because if the person smokes (when no one is at home), there will be charges for cleaning the flat when someone moves out.

Agree in advance with the other flatmates and make it very clear in the ad too.

- What are your habits or eccentricities?

When you first start living with a partner, you may learn that your partner hates clothes left on the floor, or cannot sleep with the wardrobe door open or picks his ears and then smells his fingers. There are so many habits that you will discover when you are living together.

When interviewing a flatmate, make sure you ask if they have a different habit (apart from the normal ones). If they say they are clean freaks (which is good in a way) or they like to fall asleep watching TV, this is something you should know about.

Harmonious flatsharing is when everyone is aware of the habits of their flatmates and respect them.

- Do you drink? If so, how much and how often?

If the prospective flatmate smells of alcohol, do not waste your time talking to them. You should really ask how often they drink because it will show how often they like partying, socialising (and if they bring a lot of people to the flat).

About their personal network:

- Do you have a boyfriend or a girlfriend?

This question is very important because you need to define how often the partner can stay over.

Sometimes, single people do not like the idea of sharing with couples. If you are renting a room (as a single, not as a couple) but have a partner, make sure you agree on how often the partner stays, especially if the bills are shared. This has caused arguments before (because the couple has more frequent showers and cooks more often, so the bills become more expensive).

- Do you have friends over? How often?

This should be defined as soon as you decide to invite someone to move in. Make sure you explicitly say that you do not want friends over after a certain time of the night, because you have to wake up early next morning. If you think the person will clash with the timetable of the flat, choose someone else. You will save yourself a lot of headaches if you choose the right one!

- Do you have a pet?

Most – if not all – rented properties do not allow pets. Again, specify that in your ad. If your flat allows pets, you should discuss with the future flatmates how the dynamics will work about cleanliness, walking, feeding, etc.

About sharing:

- Do you mind cleaning?

If there is a rota for the cleaning in the flat, there should be an agreement on what is supposed to be cleaned and when. If the candidate is not very keen on cleaning, ask him or her if they would pay for a cleaner instead. If there is a cleaner already in place, just share the cost.

- What's your view of sharing food without permission?

Unfortunately, some people think that sharing a house means sharing everything that is in it, including the food. If you want to start an internal war in your household, eat everyone else's food. Nothing kills the friendly atmosphere of a flatshare faster than a mouse-mate!

- Tell us what, in your opinion, is a bad flatsharing experience.

In my opinion, this could be a good way to find out what the future flatmates will be expecting from you too. It's a two way street, of course. Be prepared to hear questions back. They also need to feel they are moving into a place they will feel comfortable.

Take every opportunity to learn something new.

If you are in the process of choosing a new flatmate (or even a lodger), it's always nice to hear what people have to say about their experiences.

The experiences you are going to have are unique and every time you meet someone from a new country, that person will be an ambassador for their country. The same applies to you!

The impressions that you will leave on people are going to stay with them for a long, long time.

The other day, three of us, an Englishman, a Brazilian man and a Spanish woman, were having a conversation in a restaurant.

My idea of the Spanish was that they do not like working very much because they party too much! (I hope my Spanish friends will not kill me after reading this! I am generalizing again – and this is wrong!!!!). This is because every time I met Spanish people in London, they were always up for fun. They did not seem serious enough to me and my Spanish friend said the same about Brazilians. You see, depending on who you meet, that person is going to leave an impression on you and you will end up saying: 'Spanish are not very hard working, they like partying too much' or 'Brazilians are so crazy they do this and that . . .'

Remember that one person does not make a nation. It's not that you met one gothic English person in Camden Town that you can say 'everyone in London is gothic.'

And the more you mix with different cultures, the more you learn about them. I learned once that Asians have a dessert that is very similar to my favourite Brazilian sweet called 'pudim'. Pudim is like cream caramel in England but it's made with condensed milk. I had friends from Bangladesh and Pakistan for dinner once and I served that. They said 'we have something very similar.' I was pleasantly surprised and we talked a lot about the similarities in food.

During all these years living abroad, I have met many people and talked about many different things. One thing that I got really interested in was their opinions on other cultures. So I decided to ask them what they think of their flatmate or partner. Some of the names I've used are not their real names and the comments reflect their opinions, not mine.

You, me and other nationalities

American x British

My friend Lisa is from Washington, DC (USA) and is married to a British man. When we discussed this issue, she started talking about the key differences between them.

'My partner and I have different names for things: like pants vs. trousers, bum vs. ass, bloody vs. the 'f' word. I don't get offended when someone is shouting at me and uses the word 'bloody'; it sounds like nothing but a word but throw the 'f' word in and I am very offended.

So, communicating effectively using the right words was a huge thing between us. Between personality and culture, there is quite a bit. It seems there is a fine line between classes in Britain and it is difficult for some people to let it go. My husband is from a working class family and I guess I am from what would be a middle class family. In Britain, working class are jobs like tube drivers, retail, taxi drivers, nurses, etc. I am still not sure of the separations on that bit but he seems very pent up about that difference in us. It has taken him about 4 years to let it go.

I have learned a lot from him about the differences in areas in the UK and what is considered good and bad. Britons seem very keen on giving the history of certain things (places, objects, sayings, etc.) and things that are customary here. It is a huge relief to have someone to consult.

If I were to give advice, I would say just be yourself because a person from the UK is a little more restricted on expressing themselves. They are the king/queens of keeping it to themselves so don't let that scare you. Being from a different country gives us a sort of permission to 'act out' so go for it and don't be scared of it. I spent the first couple of years being afraid to be me and it just made me repressed. So act like you and don't try and adjust who you are for anything or anyone. Also, enjoy the area.'

Greek x French

Mark was born in London but his parents are Greek Cypriot.

'I consider myself more Greek then English because of the way I was brought up. My partner is French and the main difference between us is that the French are not as traditional with religion as Greek people are. Living with a French girl has taught me so much about food, religion and their festivals. It has brought so much knowledge about the country and its history – I would never have learnt all this at school. The variety of food (especially cheese) and wine is incredible. I learnt about the grapes and everything that goes with wine. My advice – if you live with a French person: embrace it and make the most of it. They have a lot to offer!'

Brazilian x English

Carlos has lived in Europe for 28 years. He's lived in Vienna, Berlin, Rio de Janeiro and London. He now lives in South of France with his partner. They have been together for 11 years and are now married.

'There are advantages and disadvantages in meeting someone when you are mature. We were both in our 40s when we met. The baggage is 'heavy' and you are already settled in your own way.

The English have a great sense of humour – once you learn to appreciate that. They can be very sarcastic and if you do not understand the language very well, you can get offended very easily.

The good thing about living with someone from a different country is that you will have a different view in life for everything – this can be your best friend but also your worst enemy! You need to find the balance.

My advice is to learn the language well so you can learn about their culture. Only during hours and hours of conversation will you understand why they behave that way.'

Finnish x American

Tiina is a friend of mine from Finland. She lived in Italy and London for a few years and is now married to Kevin, an American pilot. Tiina has an amazing insight about Americans, which she explains:

'I think the main differences between Finns and Americans are that Finns are more introverted than Americans. Americans are very good at "selling" themselves while Finns tend to be more humble and shy about talking about themselves. Our sense of humour is probably very different too. Finns tend to be more sarcastic and I don't think the American sense of humour is sarcastic. A lot of things I mentioned I think are the influence of culture. Finnish shyness might be a personality trait, but I think one can learn to be extrovert by being surrounded by extroverts. When you talk about the cultural differences, it is so important to remember that America has 350 million people from lots of different nationalities, while Finland is only 5 million nearly pure Finns! That makes a huge difference and puts things in different perspective.

I think it is very important for Americans to always be nice and kind to everyone, to "look good" to others while Finns perhaps don't always consider this to be so important. We tend to think that if you are always nice, you are not being genuine.

Americans like to talk about money, I was gobsmacked one time in Las Vegas where a casino dealer asked Kevin how much money he makes . . . lol! Obviously, that is something that is not asked from anyone in Finland or maybe really anywhere in Northern Europe.

Another subject we don't talk about is religion. It is a very private matter in Finland and often even people who are deeply religious won't talk about it.

And then the nudity . . . in Finland, it is not a big deal; we all have seen naked people all of our lives but in America, it is a taboo. You never see anyone naked on TV while in Finland it's just business as usual!

Another big difference is the way we celebrate Christmas. The way to celebrate Christmas over here I think is cultural since it seems to me that everyone celebrates pretty much the same way and it is very different from our Christmas celebrations in Finland. It almost seems that we are having two totally different festivities.

Since I am used to American "niceties", I must say that I like it. I think that even if it is not always genuine, I rather have that than a genuine Finn who is having a bad day and I'm happening to come to his way . . .

After all, we are all humans and it is easy to categorize people, but I think Americans have lots of good and bad in them as well as Finns do. I lived in Italy and in England quite a long time, so after that, I think America and Americans are pretty neutral people.'

Korean x German

Kim has been a friend of mine for over 10 years. She has lived with Germans and has been in a relationship with a German guy from Berlin for the past five years. When I talked to her about cultural differences, she had an amazing explanation – since she had so much experience dealing with Germans – as friends and boyfriends.

'Most people think Germans are stubborn. They are not. I think they are argumentative and as long as you show or prove to them what you talking about is true (or something along these lines), they will be on your side.

Things have to be logical to them or they will argue with you until the logic is there. Logic does not have to be about numbers, though. One example (which I learned at the very beginning with them) is if they know that draft cause colds, they will consider drafts bad. It sounds like common sense but I wanted to give an example about logical thinking without numbers being involved. Another thing they like is the room being ventilated but it does not mean they like drafts.

They also LOVE sparkling water. They drink tons of it. It's a very German thing!'

Swiss x Korean

Karen is a beautiful Swiss girl whom I met during her internship in London. We spent a few night outs together in 2004 after she had moved into our flatshare. I remember well when we talked about her former flatshare where she had Korean flatmates. Hyori was

Karen's best friend while living in the flat. Hyori was a fashion student and very techi-savvy! She was really nice. I met her a couple of times.

'I could not live with someone more different than a Korean. Their culture is so different. We talked a lot about their habits in general but the striking ones were:

Eating: in restaurants, you don't order the bill. You stand up and pay at the entrance (or exit). Also, you don't tip in Korea. People will not understand if you leave money behind.'

Drinking: Karen also learned that when they were drinking something together Hyori would never pour a drink for herself and when Karen was pouring the drink for Hyori, she would hold the glass or cup with both hands. Apparently, this is something that Koreans do when you are drinking with them. Evidently, being drunk is very acceptable in Korean culture.

Canadian x Chilean

Caroline is Canadian and has been married to her Chilean husband for the past 15 years. Caroline has an amazing knowledge about Chile since she travels and has business there.

'When I first met them, I realised that the best topics of conversation were family, work and where someone is from. Chileans are very interested in learning about other countries and travels. Just like any other nationality, talking about the parts of Chile that you have visited will impress them and they will 'love' you straight away. If you talk to Chilean women, food is the best topic. They adore their own cuisine – which is very rich in flavours.

You should avoid as much as you can compare Chile with Argentina. You may create an enemy instantly! Chileans also love football but they regret their lack of funding so their country never really wins – it is not easy having Brazil as a neighbour I suppose!

Another thing that you need to get used to with Chileans is that they laugh after they said something they think is ironic or sarcastic. What is funny for Canadians is not funny for Chilean and vice versa but I think it helps if you know the culture and the people well to understand the sarcasm behind the comment.

I do not recommend you to talk about politics too early in your conversation with people you just met. They are very fiery when talking about politics. There is a lot going on in Chile. The country is very divided politically and there is a strong polarization supporter of the established political elite (these are not so critical of Pinochet) and those who criticize and oppose - especially Pinochet. The same applies for religion and the church in Chile – they are very passionate about it.'

Sudanese x Italian

When I met Daliah for a coffee to talk about her flatmates, she immediately started talking about Italians. She had lived with so many. It is not very common for Arab people to share with other nationalities; those who choose to share do it for the experience. Daliah had an interesting view on Italians. She focused a lot on food, the habits of eating and the times.

'If you think that Italy is all about pasta, cannelloni or lasagne, you are wrong! There are dishes in Italy that won't have a tomato in it. The more you travel in Italy, the more you learn.

When you go to a restaurant in Italy (Rome especially), you soon learn that waiters are not there to entertain you. Different from my country where they come every 5 minutes to ask if everything is ok, Italians serve you and leave you alone. They do not expect you to leave as soon as the meal is over (like Chinese restaurants). They let you enjoy your food. And be prepared to pay everything in cash in Italy. Sometimes, it seems they are not a developed country at all. When you go out in a restaurant, be careful with the time you are going. If you are like the British who enjoy having dinner at 7 pm, the restaurants are going to be empty and you will think that Italians do not like the place. It's not as bad as Spain (they eat VERY late) but it's not 7pm!'

Russian x South African

Natasha and I became friends when we both did a TEFL course (Teaching English as a Foreign Language). We both had dreams to go back to our countries and teach English to our fellow countrymen! Even though we finished the course, neither of us has returned to our countries yet.

Natasha used to live with South Africans. She had a South African boyfriend who was a rugby player. Rugby is a big sport there. Natasha's comments on South Africans are:

'South Africans are very similar to the British when it

comes to talking or greeting – it has to be within their privacy or at an arm's length. Only when you become friends you can kiss and hug but until then make sure you don't invade 'their privacy', as they like to say.

South Africans also do not like showing affection in public. They are private people. The only experience that I have is with white South Africans. Apparently, it's acceptable and very common (amongst the black South Africans) to show emotions in funerals and on the street if you are angry. Avoid as much as you can talking about HIV and AIDS to them. It's a taboo there. I would recommend the film 'Taxi to Soweto', which is an amazing story that shows the weaknesses you can find in South Africa. I also read a few books with great stories, one of them is from Nelson Mandela called *Long Walk to Freedom.* If you want to learn about their society and their history.

Wikipedia description of the book: Long Walk to Freedom is an autobiographical work written by South African President Nelson Mandela, and published in 1995 by Little Brown & Co. The book profiles his early life, coming of age, education and 27 years in prison. Under the Apartheid regime, Mandela was regarded as a terrorist and jailed on the infamous Robben Island for his role as a leader of the then-outlawed ANC. He has since achieved international recognition for his leadership as president in rebuilding the country's once segregated society. The last chapters of the book describe his political ascension, and his belief that the struggle continues against apartheid in South Africa.

British x Brazilian

I was actually shocked and surprised when I heard about the way some British people think of Brazilians. As I mentioned earlier, we should be an advocate for our own country, so the impressions we leave are the ones that should last.

I have asked a few of my British friends what they think of Brazilians. Some of them have partners (boyfriend, wives, etc.), some of them have best friends and some of them are flatmates. So it was quite a good variety of relationships to pick and choose the answers from. To my surprise, some of the answers were unanimous!

'Brazilians are shallow and only think about their bodies'.

I had to explore this one because I never thought that way. Then I realised that because we are from a hot country and we do not wear a lot of clothes (most of the time), we are very body conscious, of course. Our bodies are much more exposed than my fellow British friends. Winter here lasts for 4 months (very cold) and about two months of mild cold, so you are covered most of the time; there is really no need to be so body conscious if you are not showing it, right?

'Brazilians are like the Chinese; everything has rice with it!'

I laughed and had to agree on that one. We have rice with every meal but I suppose it's like British people having potatoes. Potatoes are served with many meals (in all different forms: French fries, boiled, baked, steamed, etc.). So we have rice and they have potatoes!

'Brazilians are happier and friendlier than most nations'.

I was happy to hear that but I wanted to find out why. Through research, I learnt that apparently because of the sun and the amount of vitamins the sun help to produce (including D), Brazilians are a happy nation in general. Because people are happier, they are friendlier.

When I compare to them to people who live in Northern Europe (the UK, Scandinavia, etc.), they can be very miserable sometimes. Especially in winter. It gets dark at 4 pm, so there is no sun and it feels very sad to be in a place with no sunlight. I feel sad in London sometimes so I imagine in cities or towns around the UK and other countries where there is not so much to do like London. It must indeed be very sad.

On our Facebook homepage, we will have a special page dedicated to films and books that will help you learn about other cultures. They will be suggestions by the readers (you), so other people can learn about your country, the language and the customs there.

Access our page now and add your suggestions: facebook.com/roominthemoon

Types of relationships

Time has passed and you have become really good friends with your flatties. You've been in your new home for six months and feel like you have a 'family.'

This is the sensation you start having if you live with

people for a long time. You will cry together, watch films together, laugh, cook for each other, irritate each other and enjoy life. You will learn about each other's cultures and grow together.

There will be one flatmate in particular that you will never forget or that you don't want to move out because you are just like 'twins' or 'soul mates.' You like the same things: you love watching 'Friends' and laugh together, you go out clubbing, you cook for each other.

Sometimes you will catch yourself saying 'you are the brother or sister that I never had'.

Even if you can't completely express yourself because of the language barrier, you still love your flatmate to bits! Especially when you guys get drunk together.

Just make sure you don't end up doing something you will regret after a drunken night because that can spoil everything!

Flatmates and sex

Yes, sex can spoil things between flatmates.

I'll tell you a story.

There are 3 people involved in this story: Marcos, a young Brazilian male, 24 from Sao Paulo and a couple, Mary (30 years old) and John (32 years old).

Marcos was full of energy and very enthusiastic. He moved in with John and Mary in South London when they bought their house. They had been married for 10 years.

Mary and John had a very modern relationship in which they were allowed to see other people (but the subject was not talked about).

John was a director in a marketing company and Mary worked from home making costumes for theatre companies.

Marcos also worked from home doing online research for companies and spent almost all day on his computer.

Marcos and Mary got along really well. Marcos was initially friends with John (they met through work – Marcos was doing research for John's company).

After Marcos moved in, Mary was a much happier person. She was shy and introverted and Marcos was showing Mary how to be an extrovert.

Living with a couple is a different dynamic than living with a single person. There are more boundaries that you normally do not cross. Also, couples tend to do things together and like spending more time together.

Marcos and Mary developed a very deep friendship. Marcos was attentive and spent a lot of time with Mary. She was more creative and feeling happier overall.

Six months down the line, John found a letter that Mary wrote to Marcos that included sentences like 'the mornings we spent together . . .,' 'you show me what someone has never showed me before . . .,' and 'I like the way you do this and you do that'.

John was devastated. Mary was in love with Marcos. John found out they were having an affair.

How could they do that? Living under the same roof?

Marcos was the lodger and Mary his wife for the past 10 years.

Drama spiralled out of control and Marcos ended up being deported because his visa was expired and John did not hesitate to call immigration.

I was friends with all of them. I never heard from Mary or John again. I suppose they didn't want to keep in contact with anyone who reminded them of what had happened.

I met Mary on the tube the other day and we just smiled at each other. I knew she had to keep her distance (probably, that was the promise she made to John). I suppose they are still 'happily married.'

Well, this shows you that you do not mess around with flatmates, ok? It can get you into deep trouble and you simply do not need that while you are away (unless you love drama and do not mind being deported . . . lol).

Another sex story gone wrong

This reminds me of a beautiful Chilean friend (Marta); not only was she in trouble but she also put her flatmates in trouble.

She was having an affair with a guy from work (Tobias). He was a German married to another Chilean girl (Catalina).

Long story short: Catalina found out that Tobias was having an affair. She then found out where Marta lived and called the immigration as well. The problem is:

Marta held a European passport but her flatmates did not, so her flatmates were deported that night.

The affair ended but I suppose the flatmates never found out why they were deported (if Marta wants to live for a long time, she should never tell anyone the truth!).

Well, I suppose I don't need to give more explanations of why you should not sleep with your flatmates, do I?

Let me just tell you another funny story about flatsharing and sex!

When I started working with flatshares, I had a viewing to do. It was in the middle of the afternoon on a summer day. The house was in Clapham (south London). It was a big six-bedroom house and the top floor had two rooms (one right next to the other).

There was an Australian flatmate in the house who was a manager of a bar. I knew him and knew he would be at home because he worked in the evenings.

As I entered in the house, I could hear banging on the wall but the room was on the 3rd floor. I thought there was something wrong. I was showing the house (and the room) to another Australian girl (Australians love Clapham for some reason). As we went up, the noise got louder and louder . . .

Basically, he was having a very wild session in the middle of the afternoon and the door was not locked. I can tell you, the girl was enjoying A LOT. She was screaming so much. I just looked at the girl and we both burst out laughing. She said 'the housemates seem to have a lot of fun in this house.' We laughed and went downstairs. In the end, she took the room. I wonder why . . .

There are so many other stories that I could write a whole book about them...

Flatmates and conflict

I believe that dealing with conflict only really happens during your 'upgrade' stage. It's about being mature and considerate.

In any relationship, there will be friction and arguments. Some people will handle better than others.

If you are in a house or flat with someone who is mature enough (if person is not you), once the argument ends, there will be an apology or a 'let's talk about it' kind of conversation.

One thing that I suggest is a house meeting; this works every time and in different environments (work, love, etc.).

If you are having issues with people in the house (or even if you are not involved directly) but want the atmosphere in the house to improve, ask everyone to attend a house meeting.

I did a few while living in shared houses and the way that always works was:

- – Agree with everyone on a time to be in the living room or kitchen.
- – Everyone should be relaxed and not ready for a fight. You are there to kiss and make up!

- The meeting should have a goal; for example, we will stop eating each other's food.

- Each flatmate will have 5 minutes to say what they want. Avoid emotional words or adjectives like: the stupid person who . . ., the idiot that . . .

- State the facts and what you expect: Someone ate all my chocolate. I want this to stop today.

- One flatmate should write down what everyone is saying; once the meeting is over, print the agreement and stick it on the fridge door with a magnet or send an email to everyone (the fridge is more powerful because you are going to be reading every day).

- End the meeting with hugs, hand shaking or whatever you feel like it but make sure there is a nice atmosphere in the house.

Some people will read this and think that it's very stupid. When you live in a house with six people (or 14 like I did before), you need to have these meetings whenever you feel necessary.

People get stressed and bothered about things that you have no idea about, so clearing the air is always the best way to live in peace.

Next door neighbours

Meeting the neighbours is very important, especially if you are planning to live in the property for a long time.

I remember when I stayed in France for a short while, I really enjoyed going to the bakery around the corner in the 18th District. Everybody was so friendly; there was always a 'bonjour' here and there.

I already knew a few people in the building just by saying 'ca va' or 'bonjour'. The more you do it, the easier it gets. Say 'hi' whenever you can. Ask their names and then say 'Hi Mary' – if her name is Mary, of course!

In London, things are very different. There is a culture of not talking to your neighbour. You pretend you don't see them. They look down instead of looking at you. It's very weird but you learn that it's the culture of the whole city.

If you go to the South West or the English countryside, everyone says 'good morning' and they are very friendly. You can knock at people's doors and have a cuppa (a cup of tea) with them.

It's a completely different culture.

Find out how neighbours behave in the area where you are moving. Maybe you should take the first step and knock on their door and tell them that you have moved in. They will love that, I am sure.

Also, we always need a favour of some sort. If the postman has a large package and you are not at home, your neighbour can receive the package on your behalf and vice-versa.

When you move to another country to upgrade

During a conversation with a journalist friend of mine called Leonardo (who was a tenant and also worked for me while living in London), I was amazed at his way of describing his experiences.

This is how the conversation went . . .

Leonardo and I were in a cafe, talking about his life back in Brazil - after he had lived in London and Barcelona. I asked him about his expectations, reasons, thoughts and feelings when he left Brazil for the first time.

Leonardo said that he was 26 and had been working as a journalist in Brazil for 3 years when he decided to go abroad. He knew that to go far as a journalist, he needed to live abroad in order to have a wider vision of the world – politics, culture, behaviour, etc. He was in a stable relationship, had wonderful friends, family around and life was very stable – financially and emotionally.

Deep down, he wanted to go on a big adventure. The thoughts that were going through his mind were that it was too selfish to think that way. Why should he leave all his beloved ones behind, his career, car and dog to live his own experience?

His feelings were mixed, the excitement of going abroad, the new world ahead, the places he would see (as he had studied them) while, the same time, the sadness of leaving his home, his partner, his great friends.

Leonardo emphasized that he felt guilty about leaving. He had doubts about the unknown but said that sometimes you have to be selfish and go ahead with plans that will only benefit you. It's part of life and decisions that have to be made.

His initial plans were to travel for 2 years and then go back 'home' . . . he went back 5 years ago and it was like going back to a strange place again with familiar faces this time.

I asked him how long it took him to adapt himself to the new environment after he landed in London.

He said that it is not possible to put a date or time on a new adaptation. He said that he doesn't even know that it happened 100%. What amazed him was the insecurity in completing the simplest of the tasks – like buying a weekly metro ticket. Obviously, what makes a huge difference is the language. 'Because one does not know the language well, one cannot be sure if the task is being completed correctly.'

Soon, he learned that people have different logical ways of thinking. What influences the way they are is the way they were brought up and where. People from different countries do different things when it comes to cooking, eating, behaving in public and at home, having sex, etc.

'Everything is different! You only really feel adapted when you learn to deal with these differences. It does not mean you 'accept or agree with them;' it means that you adapt yourself to them so you can live together in peace'.

Leonardo said that even after all this process and understanding, he still did not integrate 100%. 'You can interact with them, talk, have fun but it is never the same as if you were amongst your fellow country people!'

When Leonardo decided to move from London to Barcelona, he was living in a flatshare in Bermondsey and working at londonup.com's office in South London.

I asked him if moving for the second time was the same experience and process. His answer was:

'Absolutely not! I moved to Barcelona two years after I had moved to London because I was in love. I was moving to a home where everything was already in place: a home address, the circle of friends and everything else that comes with a local resident. At this stage of my life, things were different and I was much more confident and the language (Spanish is very similar to Portuguese) was easier to learn. For the first time, I felt that I had found my 'home' and would never go back to Brazil'.

I went on to ask what he would tell a friend who is moving abroad for the first time.

He said that he believes everyone needs an experience like this at some stage in their lives. It does not matter the age. It opens your mind, makes you more tolerant and gives you a completely different perspective on how people interact and behave.

His main advice is to go abroad with open to new opportunities, open your eyes and let yourself do things that you would not normally do, just to see how it goes or works.

He said that you should not have any doubts once you are there. It's half way through already. Do not stay on the fence about anything. You will learn more if you don't!

When I asked him about being homesick, he said that the feelings again are so mixed. 'You are enjoying so much this new life: FREEDOM!!!!! '

He used this word quite a lot to describe how he felt. It seems that once you enjoy the freedom of not telling anyone what you are up to, it's difficult having to go back to anything that will remove that freedom that you gained. But the happy feelings are also mixed with the sad feelings because of the distance, the pain of not being able to hug your mum when it's her birthday, for example.

He said something quite funny about the distance:

'I wish Brazil was the next stop after Bermondsey station. It would be so much easier.

But you should not let the sadness of the distance take over or overwhelm you. You need to think of the goals you want to achieve from your trip. Be happy that you are there, sharing a house or a flat with people that will make you a better person.'

We moved on to talking about making friends. It seems that in big cities like New York, Sao Paulo, London and many others, it is quite difficult to make friends.

Everyone that has lived in a big city feels lonely at some point. It's difficult to make friends that will actually care for you as much as the ones who grew up with you, right?

Making new friends will depend on many factors like where you are working, your age group, the people who you are living with and many other social groups that you decide to hang out with.

Some people think that the English are too closed and difficult to make friends with. In my opinion, this is true to a certain extent. If you put an effort into the friendship, they will respond to this effort and once an English person becomes your friend, you can count on them for life!

Leonardo told me that it was much easier to make friends in Spain than in London. He hardly met English people in London but has a lot of Spanish friends. 'Maybe it has to do with the culture being similar and Latinos being more open as people. My friends in London were Italians, South Americans and Spanish but not so many English ones. Although I have to admit that even though it was easier to make friends in Spain, they still saw me as a foreigner'.

STAGE 5

DIRECTION

CHAPTER 5

STAY IN THE NEW COUNTRY

If you decide to stay in the new country...

Well, this stage is difficult. It's probably as hard as the decision to leave your country. The difference now is that you are more mature; you are older and wiser and you have achieved a lot while living away.

You have built a network of people around you that loves you the way you are. They love you simply because you exist.

There are experiences that you have abroad that you would never be able to have while living in your country.

One example that I can give is once when Andiara (my younger sister) explained about birthday parties when you are abroad and you do not know many people.

She said that one should be happy about having a few people around to celebrate. You learn that your birthday present is actually their presence. You don't need anything material; you just need someone there to celebrate life with you and those who are going to be around you on that special occasion will make your life happier.

I had exactly the same thoughts but I never spoke to anyone about it, until Andiara told me during her first birthday party abroad.

Only when you are experiencing this situation will you understand what we mean.

The same happens during Christmas, New Year's celebrations, etc. You will always find someone who will feel compassionate and invite you to celebrate with them when they know that you are new in the country and do not know anyone with whom to spend this time of the year.

You will feel touched and will always remember them with affection.

Now, back to the decision: should you stay or should you go back to your home country?

Well, if you are expecting me to tell how that there is a formula or something else that can help you to make this decision, I am sorry but there is not.

I made my decision to stay. I decided to stay because I built a new life, I have amazing friends who love me, support me and are there for me any time I need them.

I have developed deep roots in the UK. I have a business, a dog and a house . . . it's very hard to wake up one day and say 'that's it, I've had enough. I am going back!'

It will depend on your circumstances.

There are so many factors that will influence your decision:

- your current job
- your current relationship (if you are single, life is SO much easier!)
- if you have kids

- if you are married
- if you have a business
- if you have a house, a dog, children going to school . . .

Do you see what I mean? I cannot help you to make this decision. You need to weigh this decision yourself and see what is going to be the best for you.

Have you achieved what you had planned?

If you have, is it time to go back then?

Can you live away from your family and friends that you grew up with?

It's heart-breaking, making this decision. I suffered so much before. You feel so guilty for leaving your parents behind, for leaving friends and family.

You blame yourself for causing them pain (they miss you so much!).

But at the same time, you have made your life in the new country. You have achieved so much (that probably you would not achieve in your own country?) and you still have so much to accomplish!

Well, this is something that only you can determine. Only you can see inside yourself and judge what is best and worst.

If you decide to stay in the new country, you will not be able to see your family very frequently, nor your friends from childhood or the beach you used to see every morning on the way to work.

On the other hand, you will be able to have other things that you value for yourself:

- safety (this could be physical safety, home safety, financial safety, etc.)

- love (you may have found love and he/she does not want to move to your country yet)

- achievement (you feel that you have achieved so much and you can achieve even more, so it's better to stay in the country where you are now).

So, my advice is to wait. Think a lot. Write down all the pros and cons of living where you are compared to your home country.

Use the space below to do that. Take your time . . . reflect about this decision. It's not easy and you cannot make a decision overnight! (If you find more pros than cons, you have your answer – and vice versa!)

Living in the new country:

Pros	Cons

Return to your home country

If you know exactly how long you want to live abroad and what your goals are, great!

It will be much easier for you to deal with the return.

You need to prepare yourself, though, because you will not be the same.

You will have lived so many experiences that you have no idea how much they changed you.

Now, there is something that you need to know about that you will go through, which is not going to be easy.

It's called reverse culture shock. This is when you go back to your country after you lived abroad and you have difficulties adapting yourself to your own culture.

Andiara went through this stage when she returned to Brazil after 18 months away. The first month was very hard and she wanted to come back to London.

Living in your home country:

Pros	Cons

Now, let's explore reverse culture shock a bit more.

Reverse culture shock

When you go back to your country after a year or two of being away, you will first criticise a lot. You will compare everything with the country where you were. It's pretty normal and it's inevitable.

If you were in a developing country and moved to a developed one, the criticism is even harsher. However, when you move from a developed into a developing country, you realise how lucky you are for having all the facilities of your everyday life. You see how much easier life is in a developed country and all the things that you take for granted.

So, why do you criticise your country in the beginning?

Well, for several reasons.

The first is that things 'could be better if people did things differently.' I agree with you if you think this way but not everyone has been abroad or had the chance to do things in a different way. What you need to understand is that people have been taught – at home and at school – that you should behave in certain ways, deal with situations in certain ways, etc., etc.

These 'lessons' are passed on from generation to generation and it takes generations to change them.

There is a huge change going on in the BRIC countries at the moment (Brazil, Russia, India and China). These countries are developing faster than many others. Their citizens (the masses) understand they have the power to change the ways things are and are slowly doing so.

But you have changed faster than they have because you have gone through an experience that not many people have had.

After a few months, the criticism will stop and you will see that things 'are not so bad' and will realise that there are a lot of things that are actually better in your country than in the country where you were. This is part of the process.

Once this stage is over, you are then able to balance the good and the bad and make your mind up about everything.

That's when the rational part of your brain takes over, because you are no longer overwhelmed by emotions. The emotions when you go back are the excitement of going back, the sadness of leaving behind the friends you made, the pride you feel to have reached what you have so far and looking forward to the future.

One thing that you have to learn is that YOU will make this journey and YOUR choices will be the ones that will make a huge difference to your life.

The people that you meet along the way will define this experience. You don't feel sorry for the building you are not going to see anymore. You don't cry over the clothes you can't buy, the beautiful pictures you can't take. You cry over the friends you made and that you will no longer see on a daily basis. You cry because THE PEOPLE you met have made your journey an amazing story.

The people you meet are going to be the centre of the conversations you are going to have with your friends and family. You will be telling them when you travelled to this place with that person this and that happened.

When you understand that your story is made from other people's stories, you will be glad that those people were in your life – even for a short period of time.

How to deal with reverse culture shock

When I was doing some research to write this book and better understand what people feel and go through when they move to another country, I found out that people also go through reverse cultural shock. I didn't understand this at the beginning because I have been away from my own country for many years and I still have no intention in going back. I had spoken to people about it but no one could really explain the real meaning and feeling of it to me.

Then I found a blog written by two Australians. I found a really good explanation about culture shock so I asked their permission to add this to this book – since I have not returned home yet, I can't really comment much on the subject.

They are called Caz and Graig and have been travelling around the world for many years. I found their insights very constructive and informative.

Caz starts her story by saying 'I knew culture shock all too well'.

'Teaching in Bangkok surely had me filled with frustration at *'How they didn't get it'* for many months, and then the tears that streamed down my face in the principal's office at my new school in North Carolina,

'Why me?' I wailed. **'I just don't understand'.**

'But culture shock on coming home? Are you kidding me? **I know my own culture, what is there to be shocked about?'**

Caz continues her story . . .

'When I first came home in 1999, there was no **reverse culture shock**. I came home at the same time as many of my friends, and I met Craig soon after - **one month of celebration moved to another which safely glided me past the very difficult transition stage.** And then coming home in 2006 was when the proverbial hit the fan. I went through reverse culture shock, not knowing what it was, thinking I was in a state of complete misalignment with the world around me. **My life felt like it had fallen apart and I kind of let it, through not knowing what to do.** There was no way I was going to allow that to happen again, and so I was prepared'.

The stages (This text has been taken from Caz' blog, with her consent, of course!)

The Honeymoon

This is the utter excitement and euphoria you feel upon return home. You get to celebrate with your family and friends again, *"Oh and look my favourite Thai restaurant is still open",* **and "My God look how beautiful the beach is".**

There's always Vegemite in your cupboard, the kookaburras sing to you each morning, and *"Aren't Australians just so friendly?"* For the first month being home is a time of reconnecting bliss.

As with all honeymoons, they eventually end (even if you can stretch them out for 5 years.) and end in a big way.

The transition period – also known as the emotional wig out stage.

Mood swings, foul language, unrest, frustration, anger, depression, alienation– these feelings of helplessness come in huge waves, so bad you get seasick.

You scratch desperately at the wall to find some sort of a switch to light up the darkness, but the blackness prevails.

"Back in ... Why is it like this?... I hate ... This is so frustrating...God, Australia, your Internet is so F#### crap!! ...

Where's Trader Joe when you need it? ... I just wish I could be lying in a hammock having a beer in Laos.

On and on the voices plague you. You have become an unrecognisable monster deeply set in shock.

Here's why the shock sets in and the tools you need to have in your **reverse culture shock antidote kit** to help you through.

You are not the same.

It's not that everything around you has changed, or

that things haven't even changed slightly; it is just that you have changed dramatically. You are returning to a place where people expect you to be the same. **Every day, you are faced with confusion and pressure and there is always that feeling of not being accepted for being the new you.** People want you to be who you once were and you can't. So a lot of the time ,you hide away so you can be the real you in private; the you thst you like to be now.

Antidote:

- Accept that you are not the same. You see things with different eyes and people may not recognize this anymore. Understand that this is okay. Remain true to who you are. And if it means that some friendships change as a result, then so be it. Things change; it is the nature of life.

- **Spend time with those who accept the new you and start making new friends.** We joined the Sydney Travel Tribes group, which is full of travellers who understand us. It always feels comfortable and easy to be with them. I still enjoy hanging out with my closest friends, but it's nice to be a different me with others as well.

No one is seemingly interested.

You see the eyes glaze over and the look on peoples' faces when you begin to talk about your life overseas, until eventually you learn just to shut up and do your best to join in their conversations.

And this really hurts.

You feel as if they're not interested in your life and who you are now, and act as if you are big noting your life. But you are not. **You are just sharing your life as it has been for the last couple of years.** What else can you say? You can't make your past go away.

Your memories, your thoughts and beliefs are now connected to the experiences you had on the road. This only leads you to feel more out of place and more frustrated with being home.

Antidote:

- Understand that most of the time those you are conversing with have little understanding or connection with what you have done. They may be shutting off because they don't know what to say or how to relate to you anymore.

- **Don't make all of your conversations about your travels, but don't completely shut it off either.** It is who you are and it's important to you. You might even want to let those know that this is important and it hurts you when they don't act interested.

- **Take time to find those who have travelled like you and share your stories with them**. They get it and most of the time will delight in roaming down memory lane with you.

- **Make sure you spend time with your closest friends laughing and reminiscing about special times with them**. You will feel wonderful and it will remind you what is so great about those who you chose to leave behind for long periods of time. It will help them to realize that just because you left, and lived life without them for so long does not mean you still don't love and cherish them.

There are some things about your culture you won't like.

"TRAITOR!!!!" is what your mind screams with every negative thought you feel about your own country, but you just can't help it.

On your travels, you may have discovered other ways that you liked better or think worked better. And then you have to try and explain that to others who can only agree with one thing and this is your mind, as their eyes too shout out **"TRAITOR!!!"**

Antidote:

- For culture shock, you constantly need to repeat the mantra **"Not better or worse, just different."** You need to do the same with reverse culture shock as well. It is okay to appreciate other ways more, just don't try to fight the old ways. You can't change the goddamn Internet speed, so stop wishing you were back in the land where it is 21st century speed. Go get yourself a cuppa; by the time, you return the page should have loaded.

- **Try to adapt the old things you don't like into new.** For example, I have been struggling with having to go back to a traditional Christmas; I liked doing my own thing. So I am doing my best to make it more of a joyful occasion by attending the Carols in the Domain and having our own private time as a family during the day.

- **Look for those things you love about your country and focus on that.** I try to get to the beach as often as I can as I love Australian beaches and it helps me to forget that bloody Internet speed.

You are not travelling anymore: You slip back into the mundane where nothing is new and everything is the same.

Wrong Wrong Wrong!

There is plenty of newness in your hometown or country; you just have to look at it with new eyes. Many people remain trapped in the idea that their travels are over, almost as if life is itself.

I'll put my hand up to this one when we returned home last time. There was that sense of loss and confusion as to what I was going to do now.

Antidote:

- Start travelling in your own area. This was the biggest thing this time that helped me to slay the reverse culture shock beast. Every weekend, we jumped on a train down to Sydney to explore; we began meeting with the Sydney Travel Tribes group each month; we did the seven Bridges walk, hung out at Terrigal Beach, went moonwalking and did backpacking adventures on the Gold Coast. This helped me to see the beauty of Australia again and to breathe that travel excitement and anticipation.

- **Find a way to put into practice all you have learned from your travels.** You may start a travel blog or write a book to share your experiences, or you may even start a new career. Start new hobbies, and meet new people — anything that will bring back that sense of travel for you.

Everyone wants a piece of you.

Of course. You have just returned and everyone wants to see you, and when they do, there are the eternal questions about what you are doing next.

Next?

I'm still trying to grasp being in a different time zone, let alone come up with future plans.

You've spent the last however many years, either on your own or with your partner, only socializing with other like-minded travellers, usually at a time and place that agrees with you.

Suddenly, there are people everywhere; there are birthday parties to attend, christenings, weddings, and catch up dinners. **You feel stretched in all directions, and really you just want to crawl into the nearest hammock and shut the activity out.** It is extremely overwhelming.

Antidote:

- Take the meet ups with everyone slowly. We always came home in a mad rush as we would be on the road again shortly. This time, we were in no hurry to see anyone. This was not because we didn't want to but if we did, we knew it would set us back months. So we took it slow and steady. I didn't see some of my friends for a month after I returned. You don't need to go to every event. Take a step back and take some time out.

- **Organize one event at one destination and tell everyone you know to meet you there**. This means you get to see everyone, but you are not running to a million different parties to catch up with a million different people. Make them come to you. Remember they only have one person to catch up with you have hundreds. You have to be selfish here or Reverse Culture Shock will beat you to a pulp.

Readjustment Stage

Yes. After about 6 months of being home, you will have started to readjust. How long it actually takes depends on you and how prepared you are to deal with the onslaught of turbulent emotions that are coming.

Coming home after being away for so long is a massive readjustment, bigger than you will ever realize until you go through it.

Don't forget the life of your travels, but don't hold on too tightly to them either; that is holding onto the past, which is never a good thing because life doesn't exist there.

It's time to adapt, create a new life path, and put into good use all you learned along your travel journey.

You have to find your place once again. You may discover your place is somewhere else and that is fine. You might discover you are happy to be home and that is fine too.

If you wish to read more about Caz and Craig I recommend you read their blog. It's http://www. ytravelblog.com. Get in contact with them if you need to. They are very good at helping people.

The yo-yo effect

What I call the yo-yo effect is when someone cannot cope with the culture on either side of the ocean.

I have a friend called Michelle who has been experiencing the yo-yo effect for about six years. She moved to London in 2006 and lived there for two years. When she was finally going into Stage 4 (Upgrade), she realised it was too much for her. She was scared of the 'commitment' that a permanent job would entail and was worried she would stay stuck in the same job (and in London) forever.

Michelle decided to go back to Brazil in 2008. She went straight into culture shock mode!

I remember so well her emails and Facebook messages about her hating Brazil, the people there were like this and like that... everything was 'so different' and no one understood her anymore. Why did they change, etc... etc... The fact is that, really, nothing had changed but HER.

I suppose neither of us knew at the time about reverse

culture shock and we didn't do any research. She left Brazil after six months and returned to the UK where she lived for another three years.

She had to start again (Stage 2: Search, Find, Choose!) which wasted a lot of her time, accommodation being the most time-consuming task when you are moving abroad.

The problem is that Michelle never really felt at home. She never socialized with English people so she always felt 'like a foreigner'. Many people feel this way; I think it's a state of mind more than anything else. If you follow some of the tips from this book, I am sure you will feel more 'at home' more quickly.

I live in London and I feel completely at home. I have no issues because I was born in another country. Most of my friends are English (amongst all the 30 different nationalities that are part of my circle) and we get along well. It's really up to you on how you integrate with the society in which you are going to be living.

Michelle left London again, at the end of 2011. I feel sorry for her. She kept coming and going and never really settling down anywhere. But her yo-yo stage may have ended now; she has been in Brazil for over a year.

Make sure you do not go through this stage because life becomes more difficult. You have to say goodbye every time and you waste time moving, not only physically but also emotionally.

Saying goodbye

This is the most painful part of this process, which I am going through right now. (November 2012).

My sister Andiara, who has been with me for a year and a half is now leaving. She is going back to Brazil to complete her journey. Saying goodbye is so hard and it does not matter your age, religion, colour, gender or sexual preference. I cannot really find words to describe what I am feeling at the moment. It's almost as painful as losing someone, although of course, I know I am going to see her in a few months when I visit my parents.

Saying goodbye makes you empty. Makes you feel powerless because there is really nothing you can do. I have asked so many of my friends to describe how and what they felt in order to write this book and here I am . . . unable to do it myself.

I am feeling this pain right now, at this exact moment that I writing. I am crying like a child and there is nothing that anyone would do or say that will make me feel better. I am not going to see her on a daily basis like I did before, we will not laugh, dance, joke and cook for each other. I know we will be seeing each other on Facebook and via camera but it's not the same. Seeing someone every day and suddenly not being able to call and say 'let's have a coffee tomorrow' is difficult to accept.

The feeling of emptiness is what I feel now. My throat hurts (maybe because I am on the tube and trying not to cry so people do not stare at me). It is funny how the good memories come to my mind now. You know when they say 'you only value once you lost it;' it's not that I lost it because I didn't care – it is because is beyond my control. She will live her life now and I need to get on with mine. It seems that the older, you get the more difficult it is to accept that you are so far away. Life continues and I have to accept that it was my choice.

Unfortunately, there is not much I can advise you on saying good bye. You will go through this process both ways: when you leave your home country the first time and when you return. If you decide to stay, the goodbyes become harder and harder every time you visit them.

It is impossible to find the balance on how to handle the goodbyes. Every time you make a decision, you will have to let something else go.

It's like getting married. You choose your husband and wife and you need to let your parent's house go. You are letting go of one home in order to get another one. It is hard, I know, but we all make decisions that will have impacts on our lives as well as other people's.

The best thing to do is make sure you have the best possible time of your life with them. Enjoy the moment, learn and teach something. We are always growing and developing as human beings. Make the best you can and the best will come back to you.

Enjoy your journey – wherever you are going!

About the Author

Andre Rafael dos Santos

Rafael is a Brazilian entrepreneur who moved to London in 2001 after living for a couple of years in Sao Paulo - one of the world's largest cities. In London, he started out doing menial jobs to pay his way. Rafael decided to turn his experience of living in flatshares into a business and since 2005 he runs a successful small property company – londonup.com – that turns over £1m a year. A savvy online marketer and passionate traveller, he has visited more than 200 cities in 30 different countries, meeting many extraordinary people along the way and developing a great knowledge of different cultures.

His core values in life and business are community, integrity and excellence and these are the main reasons why Rafael decided to write this book: to help people who are going to move abroad for the first time to understand the 5 stages of this new adventure. His new business idea - roominthemoon.com - is an online community dedicated to help people who are going to move to another country.

'I want people to understand each stage of their journey abroad, conquer their fears, celebrate their achievements and live a happy life while away from their home country'.

Rafael dos Santos

Printed in Great Britain
by Amazon.co.uk, Ltd.,
Marston Gate.